THIRD EDITION

METALLICA

THE COMPLETE LYRICS

ISBN 978-1-5400-6025-9

Visit Hal Leonard Online at
www.halleonard.com

Contact us:
Hal Leonard
7777 West Bluemound Road
Milwaukee, WI 53213
Email: info@halleonard.com

In Europe, contact:
Hal Leonard Europe Limited
42 Wigmore Street
Marylebone, London, W1U 2RN
Email: info@halleonardeurope.com

In Australia, contact:
Hal Leonard Australia Pty. Ltd.
4 Lentara Court
Cheltenham, Victoria, 3192 Australia
Email: info@halleonard.com.au

INTRODUCTION

Sticks and stones will break your bones, but words will always reveal the core of a person's heart and soul. Don't let anyone tell you otherwise. Indeed, think about the power of words for a moment: Wars are fought over them; ideas are shared because of them; identities are revealed through them; and emotions are expressed, churned, and healed by them.

Metallica has recorded and released 106 original songs in their career. Each one tells a story, each one bears a personal insight (however flippant), and when looked at as a body of work, they offer a timeline of the thoughts, feelings, struggles, and triumphs as experienced by the band's chief lyricist, James Hetfield.

I can hear you chuckling. After all, "Whiplash" doesn't resonate with intellectual depth, but it fairly crackles with the young, raw energy of a band seeing out their teens—nothing much more than vim, vigor, and testosterone in the Het think tank. However, juxtapose this with the likes of "Harvester of Sorrow," "The Unforgiven," and "Bleeding Me," all rich and extremely personal accounts of childhood sorrows breeding adult confusion, and you start to get a more complete view of the emotional growth and development reflected through Metallica's career.

The rest of the band were always happy to let Hetfield write the lyrics, with co-founder Lars Ulrich sometimes helping with concepts but not much more. Never gravitating towards life's cheerier issues—note the electric chair for "Ride the Lightning," drug addiction for "Master of Puppets," and a World War I victim as described by Dalton Trumbo for "One"—the outwardly cheerful and dryly humorous Hetfield has usually asked his deeper questions of life through his lyrics.

And as the years went on, Hetfield found greater therapeutic freedom and solace in lyrical composition. The lifestyle generated by being in a multi-platinum rock band can push you to escape reality, but Hetfield always found that when he was alone with pen, paper, and solitude, there was nowhere to go. Even subconsciously, the likes of "Mama Said," "Sad but True," "The God That Failed," "The House That Jack Built," "The Thing That Should Not Be," and "The Outlaw Torn" were reflections on ideas and experiences for which he otherwise could find little tangible expression.

Hetfield was never one to go around disseminating the ideas behind his songs during interviews. He has spoken on numerous occasions about the strangeness of being raised with the Christian Science religion, but beyond that he's never been one to serve you meanings on a plate. Yet true fans saw long ago how Hetfield was continually unfolding and opening up through Metallica's lyrics, mostly to himself, but also to those who cared to notice.

Of late, this has become an altogether more visceral and apparent catharsis, brought on undoubtably by Hetfield's decision to go to rehab in 2001. The subsequent return to studio work in 2002 saw a rawer, more stripped down than ever, individual who expressed anger and question almost in a stream of consciousness. The band were invited into the lyric-writing process, too, and, with their own frustrations and self-discoveries getting some pause for lyrical consideration, *St. Anger* was a harsher, less subverted and more obvious, expulsion of such emotions, with "Some Kind of Monster" and the title track (defiantly screaming, "I need a voice to let myself/to let myself go free") being prime examples. Further to this was the introduction of Robert Trujillo on bass, a move which many argue saved the band from perhaps tipping into a void. Trujillo's personality and playing style were exactly what Metallica needed, and it is no mistake that since his arrival, the band have enjoyed an on- and off-stage renaissance within themselves. Put simply, Trujillo helped remind them why they were in the band.

And as they got (and still get!) older, there's no doubt that Metallica's musical qualities got richer. Lars Ulrich, Kirk Hammett, and James Hetfield all spent more time than ever evaluating their lives, which has led to their most cohesive, expressive, and all-encompassing album yet. *Death Magnetic* has lyrically followed the map opened up by *St. Anger*, with perhaps an even clearer and less muddied honesty (emotions were not as raw or untapped this time around, and there was a crisp immediacy to them). Hetfield once again took on all the lyrics, working closely with producer Rick Rubin both to find the "Metallica vibe" and to further express life's discoveries. The result saw some of Metallica's most powerful material in many years, and with songs like "Broken, Beat & Scarred" ("The dawn, the death, the fight to the final breath/What don't kill ya makes ya more strong") and "Cyanide" ("Say, is that rain or are they tears/That stained your concrete face for years?") Hetfield was achieving perhaps his greatest level of expression and empathy with Metallica fans yet. It all suggests that there are many lyrical journeys to be taken by both parties for years to come.

Steffan Chirazi
Editor of Metallica's fan club magazine, *So What!*

CONTENTS

KILL 'EM ALL

HIT THE LIGHTS

No life till leather
We're gonna kick some ass tonight
We got the metal madness
When our fans start screaming it's right, well alright
When we start to rock we never
Want to stop again

Hit the lights
Hit the lights
Hit the lights

We know our fans are insane
We're gonna blow this place away
With volume higher
Than anything today, the only way
When we start to rock we never
Want to stop again

Hit the lights
Hit the lights
Hit the lights

With all our screaming
We're gonna rip right through your brain
We got the lethal power
It's causing you sweet pain, oh sweet pain
When we start to rock we never
Want to stop again

Hit the lights
Hit the lights
Hit the lights

THE FOUR HORSEMEN

By the last breath the fourth
winds blow
Better raise your ears
The sound of hooves knock
at your door
Lock up your wife and children
now
It's time to wield the blade
For now you've got some
company

The Horsemen are drawing
nearer
On leather steeds they ride
They've come to take your life
On through the dead of night
With the Four Horsemen ride
Or choose your fate and die

You have been dying since the
day you were born
You know it's all been planned
The quartet of deliverance rides
A sinner once, a sinner twice
No need for confessions now
'Cause now you've got the fight
of your life

The Horsemen are drawing
nearer
On leather steeds they ride
They've come to take your life
On through the dead of night
With the Four Horsemen ride
Or choose your fate and die

Time has taken its toll on you
The lines that crack your face
Famine, your body it has torn
through
Withered in every place
Pestilence, for what you had
to endure
And what you have put others
through
Death, deliverance for you for
sure
Now there's nothing you can do

So gather 'round young
warriors now
And saddle up your steeds
Killing scores with demon
swords
Now is the death of doers of
wrong
Swing the judgement hammer
down
Safely inside armor blood guts
and sweat

The Horsemen are drawing
nearer
On leather steeds they ride
They've come to take your life
On through the dead of night
With the Four Horsemen ride
Or choose your fate and die

MOTORBREATH

Living and dying, laughing and crying
Once you have seen it you'll never be the same
Life in the fast lane is just how it seems
It's hot and it's heavy and dirty and mean

Motorbreath
It's how I live my life
I can't take it any other way
Motorbreath
The sign of living fast
It is going to take your breath away

Don't stop for nothing, it's full speed or nothing
I'm taking down, you know, whatever's in my way
Getting your kicks as you're shooting the line
Sending the shivers up and down my spine

Motorbreath
It's how I live my life
I can't take it any other way
Motorbreath
The sign of living fast
It is going to take your breath away

Those people who tell you not to take chances
They are all missing on what life's about
You only live once, so take hold of the chance
Don't end up like others, same song and dance

Motorbreath
It's how I live my life
I can't take it any other way
Motorbreath
The sign of living fast
It is going to take your breath away

JUMP IN THE FIRE

Down in the depths of my fiery home
The summons bell will chime
Tempting you and all the earth
To join our sinful kind
There's a job to be done and I'm the one
You people make me do it
Now it's time for your fate and I won't hesitate
To pull you down into this pit

So come on
Jump in the fire
So come on
Jump in the fire

With hell in my eyes and with death in my veins
The end is closing in
Feeding on the minds of man
And from their souls within
My disciples all shout to search you out
And they always shall obey
Follow me now, my child, not the meek or the mild
But do just as I say

So come on
Jump in the fire
So come on
Jump in the fire

Jump by your will or be taken by force
I'll get you either way
Trying to keep the hellfire lit
I'm stalking you as prey
Living your life as me, I am you, you see
There is part of me in everyone
So reach down, grab my hand, walk with me through the land
Come home where you belong

So come on
Jump in the fire
So come on
Jump in the fire

WHIPLASH

Late at night, all systems go,
you've come to see the show
We do our best, you're the rest,
you make it real, you know

There is a feeling deep inside
that drives you fucking mad
A feeling of a hammerhead,
you need it oh so bad

Adrenaline starts to flow
You're thrashing all around
Acting like a maniac
Whiplash

Bang your head against the
stage like you never did before
Make it ring, make it bleed,
make it really sore

In a frenzied madness with your
leather and your spikes
Heads are bobbing all around,
it's hot as hell tonight

Adrenaline starts to flow
You're thrashing all around
Acting like a maniac
Whiplash

Here onstage the Marshall noise
is piercing through your ears
It kicks your ass, kicks your face,
exploding feeling nears

Now's the time to let it rip,
to let it fucking loose
We're gathered here to be with
you 'cause this is what we
choose

Adrenaline starts to flow
You're thrashing all around
Acting like a maniac
Whiplash

The show is through, the metal's
gone, it's time to hit the road
Another town, another gig,
again we will explode

Hotel rooms and motorways,
life out here is raw
But we'll never stop, we'll never
quit, 'cause we're Metallica

Adrenaline starts to flow
You're thrashing all around
Acting like a maniac

PHANTOM LORD

Sound is ripping through
your ears
The deafening sound of
metal nears
Your body's waiting for his
whips
The taste of leather on your lips

Hear the cry of war
Louder than before
With his sword in hand
To control the land
Crushing metal strikes
On this frightening night
Fall onto your knees
For the Phantom Lord

Victims falling under chains
You hear them crying dying
pains
Fist of terror's breaking through
Now there's nothing you can do

Hear the cry of war
Louder than before
With his sword in hand
To control the land
Crushing metal strikes
On this frightening night
Fall onto your knees
For the Phantom Lord

The leather armies have
prevailed
The Phantom Lord has
never failed
Smoke is lifting from the ground
The rising volume metal sound

Hear the cry of war
Louder than before
With his sword in hand
To control the land
Crushing metal strikes
On this frightening night
Fall onto your knees
For the Phantom Lord

Fall to your knees
And bow to the Phantom Lord

NO REMORSE

No mercy for what we're doing
No thought to even what we
have done
We don't need to feel the sor-
row
No remorse for the helpless one

War without end

No remorse, no repent
We don't care what it meant
Another day, another death
Another sorrow, another breath
No remorse, no repent
We don't care what it meant
Another day, another death
Another sorrow, another breath

Blood feeds the war machine
As it eats a way across the land
We don't need to feel the sorrow
No remorse is the one command

War without end

No remorse, no repent
We don't care what it meant
Another day, another death
Another sorrow, another breath
No remorse, no repent
We don't care what it meant
Another day, another death
Another sorrow, another breath

Only the strong survive
No will to save the weaker race
We are ready to kill all comers
Like a loaded gun right at your
face

War without end

No remorse, no repent
We don't care what it meant
Another day, another death
Another sorrow, another breath
No remorse, no repent
We don't care what it meant
Another day, another death
Another sorrow, another breath

Attack

Bullets are flying
People are dying
With madness surrounding,
all hell's breaking loose
Soldiers are hounding
Bodies are mounting
Cannons are shouting to take
their abuse

With war machines going
Blood starts to flowing
No mercy given to anyone here
The furious fighting
Swords are like lighting
It all becomes frightening,
you know death is near

No remorse

SEEK & DESTROY

We're scanning the scene in the city tonight
We're looking for you to start up a fight
There's an evil feeling in our brains
But it's nothing new, you know it drives us insane

Running, on our way
Hiding, you will pay
Dying, one thousand deaths
Running, on our way
Hiding, you will pay
Dying, one thousand deaths
Searching
Seek and destroy
Searching
Seek and destroy
Searching
Seek and destroy
Searching
Seek and destroy

There is no escape and that's for sure
This is the end, we won't take any more
Say goodbye to the world you live in
You have always been taking but now you're giving

Running, on our way
Hiding, you will pay
Dying, one thousand deaths
Running, on our way
Hiding, you will pay
Dying, one thousand deaths
Searching
Seek and destroy
Searching
Seek and destroy
Searching
Seek and destroy
Searching
Seek and destroy

Our brains are on fire with the feeling to kill
And it won't go away until our dreams are fulfilled
There is only one thing on our minds
Don't try running away, 'cause you're the one we will find

Running, on our way
Hiding, you will pay
Dying, one thousand deaths
Running, on our way
Hiding, you will pay
Dying, one thousand deaths
Searching
Seek and destroy
Searching
Seek and destroy
Searching
Seek and destroy
Searching
Seek and destroy

METAL MILITIA

Thunder and lightning, the gods take revenge
Senseless destruction
Victims of fury are cowardly now
Running for safety
Stabbing the harlot to pay for her sins
Leaving the virgin
Suicide running as if it were free
Ripping and tearing

Oh, through the mist and the madness
We're trying to get the message to you
Metal militia
Metal militia
Metal militia

Chained and shadowed to be left behind
Nine and one thousand
Metal militia, for your sacrifice
Ironclad soldiers
Join or be conquered, the law of the land
What will befall you?
The metalization of your inner soul
Twisting and turning

Oh, through the mist and the madness
We're trying to get the message to you
Metal militia
Metal militia
Metal militia

We are as one, yes, we all are the same
Fighting for one cause
Leather and metal are our uniforms
Protecting what we are
Joining together to take on the world
With our heavy metal
Spreading the message to everyone here
Come let yourself go

Oh, through the mist and the madness
We're trying to get the message to you
Metal militia
Metal militia
Metal militia

RIDE THE LIGHTNING

FIGHT FIRE WITH FIRE

Do unto others as they've done to you
But what the hell is this world coming to?
Blow the universe into nothingness
Nuclear warfare shall lay us to rest

Fight fire with fire
Ending is near
Fight fire with fire
Bursting with fear

We all shall die
Time is like a fuse, short and burning fast
Armageddon's here, like said in the past

Fight fire with fire
Ending is near
Fight fire with fire
Bursting with fear

Soon to fill our lungs, the hot winds of death
The gods are laughing, so take your last breath

Fight fire with fire
Ending is near
Fight fire with fire
Bursting with fear

Fight fire with fire

Fight

RIDE THE LIGHTNING

Guilty as charged
But damn it, it ain't right
There's someone else controlling
me
Death in the air
Strapped in the electric chair
This can't be happening to me

Who made you God to say,
"I'll take your life from you"?

Flash before my eyes
Now it's time to die
Burning in my brain
I can feel the flame

Wait for the sign
To flick the switch of death
It's the beginning of the end
Sweat, chilling cold
As I watch death unfold
Consciousness my only friend

My fingers grip with fear
What am I doing here?

Flash before my eyes
Now it's time to die
Burning in my brain
I can feel the flame

Someone help me
Oh please, God help me
They are trying to take it all
away
I don't want to die

Time moving slow
The minutes seem like hours
The final curtain call I see
How true is this
Just get it over with
If this is true, just let it be

Wakened by horrid scream
Freed from this frightening
dream

Flash before my eyes
Now it's time to die
Burning in my brain
I can feel the flame

FOR WHOM THE BELL TOLLS

Make his fight on the hill in the early day
Constant chill deep inside
Shouting gun, on they run through the endless gray
On they fight, for they are right, yes, but who's to say?
For a hill, men would kill. Why? They do not know
Suffered wounds test their pride
Men of five, still alive through the raging glow
Gone insane from the pain that they surely know

For whom the bell tolls
Time marches on
For whom the bell tolls

Take a look to the sky just before you die
It's the last time he will
Blackened roar, massive roar, fills the crumbling sky
Shattered goal fills his soul with a ruthless cry
Stranger now are his eyes to this mystery
He hears the silence so loud
Crack of dawn, all is gone except the will to be
Now they see what will be, blinded eyes to see

For whom the bell tolls
Time marches on
For whom the bell tolls

FADE TO BLACK

Life, it seems, will fade away
Drifting further every day
Getting lost within myself
Nothing matters, no one else

I have lost the will to live
Simply nothing more to give
There is nothing more for me
Need the end to set me free

Things not what they used to be
Missing one inside of me
Deathly lost, this can't be real
Cannot stand this hell I feel

Emptiness is filling me
To the point of agony
Growing darkness taking dawn
I was me, but now he's gone

No one but me can save myself, but it's too late
Now I can't think, think why I should even try

Yesterday seems as though it never existed
Death greets me warm, now I will just say goodbye

TRAPPED UNDER ICE

I don't know how to live through this hell
Woken up, I'm still locked in this shell
Frozen soul, frozen down to the core
Break the ice, I can't take anymore

Freezing, can't move at all
Screaming, can't hear my call
I am dying to live
Cry out
I'm trapped under ice

Crystallized as I lay here and rest
Eyes of glass stare directly at death
From deep sleep I have broken away
No one knows, no one hears what I say

Freezing, can't move at all
Screaming, can't hear my call
I am dying to live
Cry out
I'm trapped under ice

Scream from my soul
Fate mystified
Hell forevermore

No release from my cryonic state
What is this? I've been stricken by fate
Wrapped up tight, cannot move, can't break free
Hand of doom has a tight grip on me

Freezing, can't move at all
Screaming, can't hear my call
I am dying to live
Cry out
I'm trapped under ice

ESCAPE

Feel no pain, but my life ain't easy
I know I'm my best friend
No one cares, but I'm so much stronger
I'll fight until the end

To escape from the true false world
Undamaged destiny
Can't get caught in the endless circle
Ring of stupidity

Out for my own, out to be free
One with my mind, they just can't see
No need to hear things that they say
Life's for my own, to live my own way

Rape my mind and destroy my feelings
Don't tell me what to do
I don't care now 'cause I'm on my side
And I can see through you

Feed my brain with your so-called standards
Who says that I ain't right?
Break away from your common fashion
See through your blurry sight

Out for my own, out to be free
One with my mind, they just can't see
No one to hear things that they say
Life's for my own, to live my own way

See them try to bring the hammer down
No damn chains can hold me to the ground

Life's for my own, to live my own way
Life's for my own, to live my own way

CREEPING DEATH

Slaves
Hebrews born to serve,
  to the pharaoh
Heed
To his every word, live in fear
Faith
Of the unknown one,
  the deliverer
Wait
Something must be done,
  four hundred years

So let it be written,
  so let it be done
I'm sent here by the chosen one
So let it be written,
  so let it be done
To kill the first born pharaoh son
I'm creeping death

Now
Let my people go,
  land of Goshen
Go
I will be with thee, bush of fire
Blood
Running red and strong
  down the Nile
Plague
Darkness three days long,
  hail to fire

So let it be written,
  so let it be done
I'm sent here by the chosen one
So let it be written,
  so let it be done
To kill the first-born pharaoh son
I'm creeping death

Die by my hand
I creep across the land
Killing first-born man

Die by my hand
I creep across the land
Killing first-born man

I
Rule the midnight air,
  the destroyer
Born
I shall soon be there,
  deadly mass
I
Creep the steps and floor,
  final darkness
Blood
Lamb's blood, painted doors,
  I shall pass

So let it be written,
  so let it be done
I'm sent here by the chosen one
So let it be written,
  so let it be done
To kill the first-born pharaoh son
I'm creeping death

MASTER OF PUPPETS

BATTERY

Lashing out the action, returning the reaction
Weak are ripped and torn away
Hypnotizing power, crushing all that cower
Battery is here to stay

Smashing through the boundaries, lunacy has found me
Cannot stop the battery
Pounding out aggression turns into obsession
Cannot kill the battery
Cannot kill the family, battery is found in me

Battery

Crushing all deceivers, mashing non-believers
Never-ending potency
Hungry violence-seeker feeding off the weaker
Breeding on insanity

Smashing through the boundaries, lunacy has found me
Cannot stop the battery
Pounding out aggression turns into obsession
Cannot kill the battery
Cannot kill the family, battery is found in me

Battery
Battery

Circle of destruction, hammer comes crushing
Powerhouse of energy
Whipping up a fury, dominating flurry
We create the battery

Smashing through the boundaries, lunacy has found me
Cannot stop the battery
Pounding out aggression turns into obsession
Cannot kill the battery
Cannot kill the family, battery is found in me

Battery

MASTER OF PUPPETS

End of passion play, crumbling away
I'm your source of self-destruction
Veins that pump with fear, sucking darkest clear
Leading on your death's construction

Taste me, you will see
More is all you need
You're dedicated to
How I'm killing you

Come crawling faster
Obey your master
Your life burns faster
Obey your master
Master

Master of puppets, I'm pulling your strings
Twisting your mind and smashing your dreams
Blinded by me, you can't see a thing
Just call my name, 'cause I'll hear you scream
Master
Master
Just call my name, 'cause I'll hear you scream
Master
Master

Needlework the way, never you betray
Life of death becoming clearer
Pain monopoly, ritual misery
Chop your breakfast on a mirror

Taste me you will see
More is all you need
You're dedicated to
How I'm killing you

Come crawling faster
Obey your master
Your life burns faster
Obey your master
Master

Master of puppets, I'm pulling your strings
Twisting your mind and smashing your dreams
Blinded by me, you can't see a thing
Just call my name, 'cause I'll hear you scream
Master
Master
Just call my name, 'cause I'll hear you scream
Master
Master

Master, master
Where's the dreams that I've been after?
Master, master
You promised only lies
Laughter, laughter
All I hear and see is laughter
Laughter, laughter
Laughing at my cries
Fix me

Hell is worth all that, natural habitat
Just a rhyme without a reason
Never-ending maze, drift on numbered days
Now your life is out of season

I will occupy
I will help you die
I will run through you
Now I rule you, too

Come crawling faster
Obey your master
Your life burns faster
Obey your master
Master

Master of puppets, I'm pulling your strings
Twisting your mind and smashing your dreams
Blinded by me, you can't see a thing
Just call my name, 'cause I'll hear you scream
Master
Master
Just call my name, 'cause I'll hear you scream
Master
Master

THE THING THAT SHOULD NOT BE

Messenger of fear in sight
Dark deception kills the light

Hybrid children watch the sea
Pray for father, roaming free

Fearless wretch
Insanity
He watches
Lurking beneath the sea
Great old one
Forbidden site
He searches
Hunter of the shadows is rising
Immortal
In madness you dwell

Crawling chaos underground
Cult has summoned twisted
sound

Out from ruins once possessed
Fallen city, living death

Fearless wretch
Insanity
He watches
Lurking beneath the sea
Timeless sleep
Has been upset
He awakens
Hunter of the shadows is rising
Immortal
In madness you dwell
In madness you dwell

Not dead which eternal lie
Stranger eons, death may die

Drain you of your sanity
Face the thing that should
not be

Fearless wretch
Insanity
He watches
Lurking beneath the sea
Great old one
Forbidden site
He searches
Hunter of the shadows is rising
Immortal
In madness you dwell

WELCOME HOME (SANITARIUM)

Welcome to where time
  stands still
No one leaves and no one will
Moon is full, never seems to
  change
Just labeled mentally deranged
Dream the same thing every
  night
I see our freedom in my sight
No locked doors, no windows
  barred
No things to make my brain
  seem scarred

Sleep, my friend, and you
  will see
That dream is my reality
They keep me locked up in
  this cage
Can't they see it's why my brain
  says "rage"

Sanitarium, leave me be
Sanitarium, just leave me alone

Build my fear of what's out there
Cannot breathe the open air
Whisper things into my brain
Assuring me that I'm insane
They think our heads are in
  their hands
But violent use brings violent
  plans
Keep him tied, it makes him well
He's getting better, can't
  you tell?

No more can they keep us in
Listen, damn it, we will win
They see it right, they see it well
But they think this saves us from
  our hell

Sanitarium, leave me be
Sanitarium, just leave me alone
Sanitarium, just leave me alone

Fear of living on
Natives getting restless now
Mutiny in the air
Got some death to do
Mirror stares back hard
"Kill," it's such a friendly word
Seems the only way
For reaching out again

DISPOSABLE HEROES

Bodies fill the fields I see, hungry heroes end
No one to play soldier now, no one to pretend
Running blind through killing fields, bred to kill them all
Victim of what said should be, a servant till I fall

Soldier boy, made of clay
Now an empty shell
Twenty-one, only son
But he served us well
Bred to kill, not to care
Do just as we say
Finished here. Greetings, Death,
He's yours to take away

Back to the front
You will do what I say, when I say
Back to the front
You will die when I say, you must die
Back to the front
You coward, you servant, you blind man

Barking of machine-gun fire does nothing to me now
Sounding of the clock that ticks, get used to it somehow
More a man, more stripes you wear, glory-seeker trends
Bodies fill the fields I see
The slaughter never ends

Soldier boy, made of clay
Now an empty shell
Twenty-one, only son
But he served us well
Bred to kill, not to care
Do just as we say
Finished here. Greetings, Death,
He's yours to take away

Back to the front
You will do what I say, when I say
Back to the front
You will die when I say, you must die
Back to the front
You coward, you servant, you blind man

Why am I dying?
Kill, have no fear
Lie, live off lying
Hell, hell is here

I was born for dying

Life planned out before my birth, nothing could I say
Had no chance to see myself, molded day by day
Looking back I realize, nothing have I done
Left to die with only friend
Alone I clench my gun

Soldier boy, made of clay
Now an empty shell
Twenty-one, only son
But he served us well
Bred to kill, not to care
Just do as we say
Finished here. Greetings, Death,
He's yours to take away

Back to the front
You will do what I say, when I say
Back to the front
You will die when I say, you must die
Back to the front
You coward, you servant, you blind man

Back to the front

LEPER MESSIAH

Spineless from the start
Sucked into the part
Circus comes to town
You play the lead clown

Please, please
Spreading his disease,
  living by his story
Knees, knees
Falling to your knees,
  suffer for his glory
You will

Time for lust, time for lie
Time to kiss your life goodbye
Send me money, send me green,
  heaven you will meet
Make a contribution and you'll
  get the better seat

Bow to Leper Messiah

Marvel at his tricks
Need your Sunday fix
Blind devotion came
Rotting your brain

Chain, chain
Join the endless chain, taken by
  his glamour
Fame, fame
Infection is the game, stinking
  drunk with power
We see

Time for lust, time for lie
Time to kiss your life goodbye
Send me money, send me green,
  heaven you will meet
Make a contribution and you'll
  get the better seat

Bow to Leper Messiah

Witchery, weakening
Sees the sheep are gathering
Set the trap, hypnotize
Now you follow

Time for lust, time for lie
Time to kiss your life goodbye
Send me money, send me green,
  heaven you will meet
Make a contribution and you'll
  get the better seat

Lie

DAMAGE, INC.

Dealing out the agony within
Charging hard and no one's
gonna give in
Living on your knees, conformity
Or dying on your feet for
honesty
Inbred, our bodies work as one
Bloody, but never cry submission
Following our instinct,
not a trend
Go against the grain until
the end

Blood will follow blood
Dying time is here
Damage, Incorporated

Slamming through, don't fuck
with razorback
Stepping out? You'll feel our hell
on your back
Blood follows blood and we
make sure
Life ain't for you and we're
the cure
Honesty is my only excuse
Try to rob us of it, but it's no use
Steamroller action crushing all
Victim is your name and you
shall fall

Blood will follow blood
Dying time is here
Damage, Incorporated

We chew and spit you out
We laugh, you scream and shout
All flee, with fear you run
You'll know just where we
come from
Damage, Incorporated

Damage jackals ripping right
through you
Sight and smell of this,
it gets me going
Know just how to get just what
we want
Tear it from your soul in nightly
hunt
Fuck it all and fucking no regrets
Never happy endings on these
dark sets
All's fair for Damage, Inc.
you see
Step a little closer, if you please

Blood will follow blood
Dying time is here
Damage, Incorporated

...AND JUSTICE FOR ALL

BLACKENED

Blackened is the end
Winter it will send
Throwing all you see
Into obscurity

Death of Mother Earth
Never a rebirth
Evolution's end
Never will it mend

Never

Fire
To begin whipping dance
of the dead
Blackened is the end
To begin whipping dance
of the dead
Color our world blackened

Blistering of earth
Terminate its worth
Deadly nicotine
Kills what might've been

Callous, frigid chill
Nothing left to kill
Never seen before
Breathing nevermore

Never

Fire
To begin whipping dance
of the dead
Blackened is the end
To begin whipping dance
of the dead
Color our world blackened

Blackened

Opposition, contradiction,
premonition, compromise
Agitation, violation,
mutilation, planet dies
Darkest color
Blistered earth
True death of life

Termination, expiration,
cancellation, human race
Expectation, liberation,
population laid to waste
See our mother
Put to death
See our mother die

Smoldering decay
Take her breath away
Millions of our years
In minutes disappears

Darkening in vain
Decadence remains
All is said and done
Never is the sun

Never

Fire
To begin whipping dance
of the dead
Blackened is the end
To begin whipping dance
of the dead
Fire
Is the outcome of hypocrisy
Darkest potency
In the exit of humanity
Color our world blackened

Blackened

...AND JUSTICE FOR ALL

Halls of justice painted green
Money talking
Power wolves beset your door
Hear them stalking
Soon you'll please their appetite
They devour
Hammer of justice crushes you
Overpower

The ultimate in vanity
Exploiting their supremacy
I can't believe the things you say
I can't believe, I can't believe the
price you pay
Nothing can save you

Justice is lost
Justice is raped
Justice is gone
Pulling your strings
Justice is done
Seeking no truth
Winning is all
Find it so grim, so true, so real

Apathy their stepping stone
So unfeeling
Hidden deep animosity
So deceiving
Through your eyes their light
burns
Hoping to find
Inquisition sinking you
With prying minds

The ultimate in vanity
Exploiting their supremacy
I can't believe the things you say
I can't believe, I can't believe the
price you pay
Nothing can save you

Justice is lost
Justice is raped
Justice is gone
Pulling your strings
Justice is done
Seeking no truth
Winning is all
Find it so grim, so true, so real

Lady Justice has been raped
Truth assassin
Rolls of red tape seal your lips
Now you're done in

Their money tips her scales again
Make your deal
Just what is truth, I cannot tell
Cannot feel

The ultimate in vanity
Exploiting their supremacy
I can't believe the things you say
I can't believe, I can't believe the
price we pay
Nothing can save us

Justice is lost
Justice is raped
Justice is gone
Pulling your strings
Justice is done
Seeking no truth
Winning is all
Find it so grim, so true, so real

Seeking no truth
Winning is all
Find it so grim, so true, so real

EYE OF THE BEHOLDER

Do you see what I see?
Truth is an offence
Your silence for your confidence

Do you hear what I hear?
Doors are slamming shut
Limit your imagination, keep you where they must

Do you feel what I feel?
Bittering distress
Who decides what you express?

Do you take what I take?
Endurance is the word
Moving back instead of forward seems to me absurd

Doesn't matter what you see
Or into it what you read
You can do it your own way
If it's done just how I say

Independence limited
Freedom of choice
Choice is made for you, my friend
Freedom of speech
Speech is words that they will bend
Freedom with their exception

Do you fear what I fear?
Living properly
Truths to you are lies to me

Do you choose what I choose?
More alternatives
Energy derives from both the plus and negative

Do you need what I need?
Boundaries overthrown
Look inside, to each his own

Do you trust what I trust?
Me, myself, and I
Penetrate the smoke screen, I see through the selfish lie

Doesn't matter what you see
Or into it what you read
You can do it your own way
If it's done just how I say

Independence limited
Freedom of choice
Choice is made for you, my friend
Freedom of speech
Speech is words that they will bend
Freedom with their exception

Do you know what I know?
Your money and your wealth
Your silence just to hear yourself

Do you want what I want?
Desire not a thing
I hunger after independence, lengthen freedom's ring

Doesn't matter what you see
Or into it what you read
You can do it your own way
If it's done just how I say

Independence limited
Freedom of choice
Choice is made for you, my friend
Freedom of speech
Speech is words that they will bend
Freedom no longer for you

Doesn't matter what you see
Or into it what you read
You can do it your own way
If it's done just how I say

ONE

I can't remember anything
Can't tell if this is true or dream
Deep down inside I feel to
scream
This terrible silence stops me

Now that the war is through
with me
I'm waking up, I cannot see
That there is not much left of me
Nothing is real but pain now

Hold my breath as I wish for
death
Oh please, God, wake me

Back in the womb it's much
too real
In pumps life that I must feel
But can't look forward to reveal
Look to the time when I'll live

Fed through the tube that
sticks in me
Just like a wartime novelty
Tied to machines that make
me be
Cut this life off from me

Hold my breath as I wish
for death
Oh please, God, wake me

Now the world is gone,
I'm just one
Oh God, help me
Hold my breath as I wish
for death
Oh please, God, help me

Darkness imprisoning me
All that I see
Absolute horror
I cannot live
I cannot die
Trapped in myself
Body my holding cell

Landmine has taken my sight
Taken my speech
Taken my hearing
Taken my arms
Taken my legs
Taken my soul
Left me with life in hell

THE SHORTEST STRAW

Suspicion is your name
Your honesty to blame
Put dignity to shame
Dishonor
Witch-hunt modern day
Determining decay
The blatant disarray
Disfigure
The public eye's disgrace
Defying common place
Unending paper chase
Unending

Deafening
Painstaking
Reckoning
This vertigo it doth bring

Shortest straw
Challenge liberty
Downed by law
Live in infamy
Rub you raw
Witch-hunt riding through
Shortest straw
The shortest straw has been
pulled for you

Pulled for you
Shortest straw
Pulled for you
Shortest straw
Pulled for you
Shortest straw
The shortest straw has been
pulled for you

The accusations fly
Discrimination, why?
Your inner self to die
Intruding
Doubt sunk itself in you
Its teeth and talons through
You're living Catch 2-2
Deluding
A mass hysteria
A megalomania
Reveal dementia
Reveal

Secretly
Silently
Certainly
In vertigo you will be

Shortest straw
Challenge liberty
Downed by law
Live in infamy
Rub you raw
Witch-hunt riding through
Shortest straw
This shortest straw has been
pulled for you

Pulled for you
Shortest straw
Pulled for you
Shortest straw
Pulled for you
Shortest straw
Shortest straw has been
pulled for you

Shortest straw
Pulled for you
Shortest straw
Pulled for you
Shortest straw
Pulled for you
Shortest straw
Shortest straw has been
  pulled for you

Behind you, hands are tied
Your being, ostracized
Your hell is multiplied
Upending
The fallout has begun
Oppressive damage done
Your many turned to none
To nothing
You're reaching your nadir
Your will has disappeared
The lie is crystal clear
Defending

Channels red
One word said
Blacklisted
With vertigo make you dead

Shortest straw
Challenge liberty
Downed by law
Live in infamy
Rub you raw
Witch-hunt riding through
Shortest straw
The shortest straw has been
  pulled for you
Pulled for you

HARVESTER OF SORROW

My life suffocates
Planting seeds of hate
I've loved, turned to hate
Trapped far beyond my fate

I give, you take
This life that I forsake
Been cheated of my youth
You turned this lie to truth

Anger, misery
You'll suffer unto me

Harvester of sorrow
Language of the mad
Harvester of sorrow

Pure black, looking clear
My work is done soon here
Try getting back to me
Get back which used to be

Drink up
Shoot in
Let the beatings begin
Distributor of pain
Your loss becomes my gain

Anger
Misery
You'll suffer unto me

Harvester of sorrow
Language of the mad
Harvester of sorrow

All have said their prayers
Invade their nightmares
To see into my eyes
You'll find where murder lies

Infanticide

Harvester of sorrow
Language of the mad
Harvester of sorrow
Language of the mad
Harvester of sorrow

THE FRAYED ENDS OF SANITY

Never hunger
Never prosper
I have fallen prey to failure

Struggle within
Triggered again
Now the candle burns at
both ends

Twisting under schizophrenia
Falling deep into dementia

Old habits reappear
Fighting the fear of fear
Growing conspiracy
Everyone's after me
Frayed ends of sanity
Hear them calling
Hear them calling me

Birth of terror
Death of much more
I'm the slave of fear, my captor

Never warnings
Spreading its wings
As I wait for the horror she
brings

Loss of interest, question,
wonder
Waves of fear they pull
me under

Old habits reappear
Fighting the fear of fear
Growing conspiracy
Everyone's after me
Frayed ends of sanity
Hear them calling
Hear them calling me

Into ruin
I am sinking
Hostage of this nameless feeling

Hell is set free
Flooded I'll be
Feel the undertow inside me

Height, hell, time, haste, terror,
tension
Life, death, want, waste, mass
depression

Old habits reappear
Fighting the fear of fear
Growing conspiracy
Myself is after me
Frayed ends of sanity
Hear them calling
Frayed ends of sanity
Hear them calling
Hear them calling me

TO LIVE IS TO DIE

When a man lies
He murders some part of the world
These are the pale deaths which men miscall their lives
All this I cannot bear to witness any longer
Cannot the kingdom of salvation take me home?

DYERS EVE

Dear Mother
Dear Father
What is this hell you have put
me through?
Believer
Deceiver
Day in, day out, live my life
through you
Pushed onto me what's wrong
or right
Hidden from this thing that
they call "life"

Dear Mother
Dear Father
Every thought I'd think you'd
disapprove
Curator
Dictator
Always censoring my every move
Children are seen but are not
heard
Tear out everything inspired

Innocence
Torn from me without your
shelter
Barred reality
I'm living blindly

Dear Mother
Dear Father
Time has frozen still what's
left to be
Hear nothing
Say nothing
Cannot face the fact I think
for me
No guarantee, it's life as-is
But damn you for not giving
me my chance

Dear Mother
Dear Father
You've clipped my wings before
I learned to fly
Unspoiled
Unspoken
I've outgrown that fucking
lullaby
Same thing I've always heard
from you,
"Do as I say, not as I do"

Innocence
Torn from me without your
shelter
Barred reality
I'm living blindly

I'm in hell without you
Cannot cope without you two
Shocked at the world that I see
Innocent victim,
please rescue me

Dear Mother
Dear Father
Hidden in your world you've
made for me
I'm seething
I'm bleeding
Ripping wounds in me that never
heal
Undying spite I feel for you
Living out this hell you
always knew

METALLICA

ENTER SANDMAN

Say your prayers, little one
Don't forget, my son,
To include everyone

Tuck you in, warm within
Keep you free from sin
Till the sandman he comes

Sleep with one eye open
Gripping your pillow tight

Exit: light
Enter: night
Take my hand
We're off to never-never land

Something's wrong, shut
the light
Heavy thoughts tonight
And they aren't of Snow White

Dreams of war, dreams of liars
Dreams of dragon's fire
And of things that will bite

Sleep with one eye open
Gripping your pillow tight

Exit: light
Enter: night
Take my hand
We're off to never-never land

Now I lay me down to sleep
Pray the Lord my soul to keep
If I die before I wake
Pray the Lord my soul to take

Hush little baby, don't say
a word
And never mind that noise you
heard
It's just the beasts under your
bed
In your closet, in your head

Exit: light
Enter: night
Grain of sand

Exit: light
Enter: night
Take my hand
We're off to never-never land

SAD BUT TRUE

Hey
I'm your life
I'm the one who takes you there
Hey
I'm your life
I'm the one who cares
They
They betray
I'm your only true friend now
They
They'll betray
I'm forever there

I'm your dream, make you real
I'm your eyes when you must steal
I'm your pain when you can't feel
Sad but true

I'm your dream, mind astray
I'm your eyes while you're away
I'm your pain while you repay
You know it's sad but true

You
You're my mask
You're my cover, my shelter
You
You're my mask
You're the one who's blamed
Do
Do my work
Do my dirty work, scapegoat
Do
Do my deeds
For you're the one who's shamed

I'm your dream, make you real
I'm your eyes when you must steal
I'm your pain when you can't feel
Sad but true

I'm your dream, mind astray
I'm your eyes while you're away
I'm your pain while you repay
You know it's sad but true

I'm your dream
I'm your eyes
I'm your pain
You know it's sad but true

Hate
I'm your hate
I'm your hate when you want love
Pay
Pay the price
Pay, for nothing's fair
Hey
I'm your life
I'm the one who took you here
Hey
I'm your life
And I no longer care

I'm your dream, make you real
I'm your eyes when you must steal
I'm your pain when you can't feel
Sad but true

I'm your truth, telling lies
I'm your reasoned alibis
I'm inside, open your eyes
I'm you

Sad but true

HOLIER THAN THOU

No more
The crap rolls out your mouth again
Haven't changed, your brain is still gelatin
Little whispers circle around your head
Why don't you worry about yourself instead?

Who are you? Where ya been? Where ya from?
Gossip burning on the tip of your tongue
You lie so much you believe yourself
Judge not lest ye be judged yourself

Holier than thou
You are
Holier than thou
You are

You know not

Before you judge me, take a look at you
Can't you find something better to do?
Point the finger, slow to understand
Arrogance and ignorance go hand in hand

It's not who you are, it's who you know
Others' lives are the basis of your own
Burn your bridges and build them back with wealth
Judge not lest ye be judged yourself

Holier than thou
You are
Holier than thou
You are

You know not

Who the hell are you?

THE UNFORGIVEN

New blood joins this earth
And quickly he's subdued
Through constant pained
disgrace
The young boy learns their rules

With time, the child draws in
This whipping boy done wrong
Deprived of all his thoughts
The young man struggles on
and on, he's known
A vow unto his own
That never from this day
His will they'll take away

What I've felt
What I've known
Never shined through in what
I've shown
Never be
Never see
Won't see what might have
been

What I've felt
What I've known
Never shined through in what
I've shown
Never free
Never me
So I dub thee "Unforgiven"

They dedicate their lives
To running all of his
He tries to please them all
This bitter man he is

Throughout his life the same
He's battled constantly
This fight he cannot win
A tired man they see no longer
cares
The old man then prepares
To die regretfully
That old man here is me

What I've felt
What I've known
Never shined through in what
I've shown
Never be
Never see
Won't see what might have
been

What I've felt
What I've known
Never shined through in what
I've shown
Never free
Never me
So I dub thee "Unforgiven"

You labeled me
I'll label you
So I dub thee "Unforgiven"

WHEREVER I MAY ROAM

...And the road becomes my
  bride
I have stripped of all but pride
So in her I do confide
And she keeps me satisfied
Gives me all I need

...And with dust in throat I crave
Only knowledge will I save
To the game you stay a slave
Rover, wanderer
Nomad, vagabond
Call me what you will

But I'll take my time anywhere
Free to speak my mind anywhere
And I'll redefine anywhere

Anywhere I roam
Where I lay my head is home

...And the earth becomes my
  throne
I adapt to the unknown
Under wandering stars I've
  grown
By myself but not alone
I ask no one

...And my ties are severed clean
The less I have, the more I gain
Off the beaten path I reign
Rover, wanderer
Nomad, vagabond
Call me what you will

But I'll take my time anywhere
I'm free to speak my mind
  anywhere
And I'll never mind anywhere

Anywhere I roam
Where I lay my head is home

But I'll take my time anywhere
I'm free to speak my mind
And I'll take my find anywhere

Anywhere I roam
Where I lay my head is home

Carved upon my stone
My body lie, but still I roam
Wherever I may roam
Wherever I may roam
Wherever I may roam

DON'T TREAD ON ME

Liberty or death, what we so
proudly hail
Once you provoke her, rattling
of her tail
Never begins it, never, but once
engaged
Never surrenders, showing the
fangs of rage

Don't tread on me

So be it
Threaten no more
To secure peace is to prepare
for war
So be it
Settle the score
Touch me again for the words
that you will hear evermore

Don't tread on me

Love it or live it, she with the
deadly bite
Quick is the blue tongue, forked
as the lighting strike
Shining with brightness, always
on surveillance
The eyes, they never close,
emblem of vigilance

Don't tread on me

So be it
Threaten no more
To secure peace is to prepare
for war
So be it
Settle the score
Touch me again for the words
that you will hear evermore

Don't tread on me

So be it
Threaten no more
To secure peace is to prepare
for war

Liberty or death, what we so
proudly hail
Once you provoke her, rattling
of her tail

So be it
Threaten no more
To secure peace is to prepare
for war
So be it
Settle the score
Touch me again for the words
that you will hear evermore

Don't tread on me

THROUGH THE NEVER

All that is, was and will be
Universe much too big to see

Time and space never ending
Disturbing thoughts, questions
pending
Limitations of human
understanding
Too quick to criticize
Obligation to survive
We hunger to be alive

All that is, ever
Ever was
Will be ever
Twisting
Turning
Through the never

In the dark, see past our eyes
Pursuit of truth no matter where
it lies

Gazing up to the breeze of the
heavens
On a quest, meaning, reason
Came to be, how it begun
All alone in the family of the sun
Curiosity teasing everyone
On our home, third stone from
the sun

All that is, ever
Ever was
Will be ever
Twisting
Turning
Through the never

On through the never
We must go
On through the never
Out to the
Edge of forever
We must go
On through the never
Then never comes

All that is, ever
Ever was
Will be ever
Twisting
Turning
Who we are
Ask forever
Twisting
Turning
Through the never

Never

NOTHING ELSE MATTERS

So close no matter how far
Couldn't be much more from
the heart
Forever trusting who we are
And nothing else matters

Never opened myself this way
Life is ours, we live it our way
All these words I don't just say
And nothing else matters

Trust I seek and I find in you
Every day for us something new
Open mind for a different view
And nothing else matters

Never cared for what they do
Never cared for what they know
But I know

So close no matter how far
It couldn't be much more from
the heart
Forever trusting who we are
And nothing else matters

Never cared for what they do
Never cared for what they know
But I know

I never opened myself this way
Life is ours, we live it our way
All these words I don't just say
And nothing else matters

Trust I seek and I find in you
Every day for us something new
Open mind for a different view
And nothing else matters

Never cared for what they say
Never cared for games they play
Never cared for what they do
Never cared for what they know
And I know

So close no matter how far
Couldn't be much more from
the heart
Forever trusting who we are
No, nothing else matters

OF WOLF AND MAN

Off through the new day's mist I run
Out from the new day's mist I have come
I hunt
Therefore I am
Harvest the land
Taking of the fallen lamb

Off through the new day's mist I run
Out from the new day's mist I have come
We shift
Pulsing with the earth
Company we keep
Roaming the land while you sleep

Shape shift, nose to the wind
Shape shift, feeling I've been
Move swift, all senses clean
Earth's gift, back to the meaning of life

Bright is the moon, high in starlight
Chill in the air, cold as steel tonight
We shift
Call of the wild
Fear in your eyes
It's later than you realized

Shape shift, nose to the wind
Shape shift, feeling I've been
Move swift, all senses clean
Earth's gift, back to the meaning of life

I feel a change
Back to a better day
Hair stands on the back of my neck
In wildness is the preservation of the world
So seek the wolf in thyself

Shape shift, nose to the wind
Shape shift, feeling I have been
Move swift, all senses clean
Earth's gift
Back to the meaning of wolf and man

THE GOD THAT FAILED

Pride you took
Pride you feel
Pride that you felt when
 you'd kneel

Not the word
Not the love
Not what you thought from
 above

It feeds
It grows
It clouds all that you will know
Deceit
Deceive
Decide just what you believe

I see faith in your eyes
Never you hear the
 discouraging lies
I hear faith in your cries
Broken is the promise, betrayal
The healing hand held back by
 the deepened nail
Follow the god that failed

Find your peace
Find your say
Find the smooth road on
 your way

Trust you gave
A child to save
Left you cold and him in grave

It feeds
It grows
It clouds all that you will know
Deceit
Deceive
Decide just what you believe

I see faith in your eyes
Never you hear the
 discouraging lies
I hear faith in your cries
Broken is the promise, betrayal
The healing hand held back by
 the deepened nail
Follow the god that failed

I see faith in your eyes
Broken is the promise, betrayal
The healing hand held back by
 the deepened nail
Follow the god that failed

Pride you took
Pride you feel
Pride that you felt when
 you'd kneel

Trust you gave
A child to save
Left you cold and him in grave

I see faith in your eyes
Never you hear the
 discouraging lies
I hear faith in your cries
Broken is the promise, betrayal
The healing hand held back by
 the deepened nail
Follow the god that failed
Follow the god that failed
Broken is the promise, betrayed
Betrayal

MY FRIEND OF MISERY

You just stood there screaming
Fearing no one was listening to you
They say the empty can rattles the most
The sound of your own voice must soothe you
Hearing only what you want to hear
And knowing only what you've heard
You, you're smothered in tragedy
And you're out to save the world

Misery
You insist that the weight of the world
Should be on your shoulders
Misery
There's much more to life than what you see
My friend of misery

You still stood there screaming
No one caring about these words you tell
My friend, before your voice is gone
One man's fun is another's hell
These times are sent to try men's souls
But something's wrong with all you see
You, you'll take it on all yourself
Remember, misery loves company

Misery
You insist that the weight of the world
Should be on your shoulders
Misery
There's much more to life than what you see
My friend of misery

You just stood there screaming
My friend of misery

THE STRUGGLE WITHIN

Reaching out for something
you've got to feel
While clutching to what you had
thought was real

Kicking at a dead horse
pleases you
No way of showing your
gratitude
So many things you don't
want to do
What is it? What have you
got to lose?

What the hell?
What is it you think you're
gonna find?
Hypocrite
Boredom sets into the boring
mind

Struggle within, it suits you fine
Struggle within, your ruin
Struggle within, you seal your
own coffin
Struggle within, the struggling
within

Home is not a home, it becomes
a hell
Turning it into your prison cell
Advantages are taken,
not handed out
While you struggle inside your
hell

Reaching out
Grabbing for something you've
got to feel
Closing in
The pressure upon you is so
unreal

Struggle within, it suits you fine
Struggle within, your ruin
Struggle within, you seal your
own coffin
Struggle within,
struggling within

Struggle

Reaching out for something
you've got to feel
While clutching to what you had
thought was real

What the hell?
What is it you think you're
gonna find?
Hypocrite
Boredom sets into the boring
mind

Struggle within, it suits you fine
Struggle within, your ruin
Struggle within, you seal your
own coffin
Struggle within,
struggling within

LOAD

AIN'T MY BITCH

Outta my way
Outta my day
Out of your mind and into mine

Into no one
Into not one
Into your step but out of time

Headstrong
What's wrong?
I've already heard this song
before
You arrived, but now it's time to
kiss your ass goodbye

Dragging me down
Why you around?
So useless

It ain't my fall
It ain't my call
It ain't my bitch
It ain't my bitch

Down on the sun
Down and no fun
Down and out, where the hell
you been?

Damn it all down
Damn it unbound
Damn it all down to hell again

Stand tall
Can't fall
Never even bend at all before
You arrived, but now it's time to
kiss your ass goodbye

Dragging me down
Why you around?
So useless

It ain't my fall
It ain't my call
It ain't my bitch

Outta my way

Outta my way
Outta my day
Out of your mind and into mine

Into no one
Into not one
Into your step but out of time

Headstrong
What's wrong?
I've already heard this song
before
You arrived, but now it's time to
kiss your ass goodbye
And now it's time to kiss your
ass goodbye

Dragging me down
While you around?
So useless

It ain't my fall
It ain't my call
It ain't my bitch

No way but down
Why you're around
No fooling

It ain't my smile
It ain't my style
It ain't my bitch
Oh, it ain't mine

Ain't mine
Your kind
You're stepping out of time

Ain't mine
Your kind
You're stepping out of time

Taking me down
Why you around
No fooling

It ain't my fall
It ain't my call
It ain't my bitch
You ain't mine

2 X 4

I'm gonna make you, shake you,
 take you
I'm gonna be the one who
 breaks you
Put the screws to you, yeah, my
 way
Yeah, come on and come on,
 come and make my day
Make my day

Got some hell to pay, I steal
 your thunder
The joy of violent movement,
 pulls you under
Bite the bullet, well hard
Yeah, but I die harder,
 so go too far
Too far

Friction, fusion, retribution
I can't hear you, talk to me
I can't hear you, so talk to me
I can't hear you,
 are you talking to me?
I can't hear you,
 are you talking to me?
I can't hear you,
 time to meet my lord
I can't hear you,
 talk to two by four

I'm gonna make you, shake you,
 take you
I'm gonna be that one who
 breaks you
Put the screws to you, my way
Hey, come on and come on,
 come and make my day
Make my day

Friction, fusion, retribution
I can't hear you, talk to me
I can't hear you, come talk to me
I can't hear you,
 are you talking to me?
I can't hear you,
 are you talking to me?
I can't hear you,
 time to meet my lord
I can't hear you,
 talk to two by four

Talk to two by four
It don't take no more

Friction, fusion, retribution
I'm gonna make you talk to me
I'm gonna trick you,
 so talk to me
I can't hear you,
 are you talking to me?
I can't hear you,
 you talking to me?
I can't hear you,
 time to meet my lord
I can't hear you,
 talk to two by four
She don't take no more

THE HOUSE JACK BUILT

Open door, so I walk inside
Close my eyes, find my place
to hide
And I shake as I take it in
Let the show begin

Open my eyes just to have them
close again
Well on my way, but on my way
to where I've been
It swallows me as it takes me in
its fog
I twist away as I give this world
the nod

Open door, so I walk inside
Close my eyes, find my place
to hide
And I shake as I take it in
Let the show begin

Open my eyes just to have them
closed once again
Don't want control
As it takes me down and down
and down again
Is that the moon or just a light
that lights this dead-end
street?
Is that you there or just another
demon that I meet?

The higher you are
The farther you fall
The longer the walk
The farther you crawl
My body, my temple
This temple, it tilts
Step into the house that
Jack built

The higher you are
The farther you fall
The longer the walk
The farther you crawl
My body, my temple
This temple, it tilts
Yes, this is the house that
Jack built

Open door, yes, I walk inside
Swallow me so the pain subsides
And I shake as I take the sin
Let the show begin

The higher you are
The farther you fall
The longer the walk
The farther you crawl
My body, my temple
This temple, it tilts
Yes, this is the house that
Jack built

The higher you are
The farther you fall
The longer the walk
The farther you crawl
My body, my temple
This temple, it tilts
Yes, I am, I am, I am

Open my eyes
It swallows me
Is that you there
I twist away
Away
Away
Away

UNTIL IT SLEEPS

Where do I take this pain
  of mine?
I run, but it stays right by my side

So tear me open, pour me out
There's things inside that scream
  and shout
And the pain still hates me
So hold me until it sleeps

Just like the curse,
  just like the stray
You feed it once and
  now it stays
Now it stays

So tear me open but beware
There's things inside without
  a care
And the dirt still stains me
So wash me until I'm clean

It grips you, so hold me
It stains you, so hold me
It hates you, so hold me
It holds you, so hold me
Until it sleeps

So tell me why you've
  chosen me
Don't want your grip,
  don't want your greed
Don't want it

I'll tear me open,
  make you gone
No more can you hurt anyone
And the fear still shakes me
So hold me until it sleeps

It grips you, so hold me
It stains you, so hold me
It hates you, so hold me
It holds you, holds you,
  holds you until it sleeps

I don't want it

So tear me open but beware
There's things inside without
  a care
And the dirt still stains me
So wash me till I'm clean

I'll tear me open,
  make you gone
No longer will you hurt anyone
And the hate still shapes me
So hold me until it sleeps
Until it sleeps

KING NOTHING

Wish I may, wish I might
Have this I wish tonight
Are you satisfied?
Dig for gold, dig for fame
You dig to make your name
Are you pacified?

All the wants you waste
All the things you've chased

Then it all crashes down
And you break your crown
And you point your finger
But there's no one around
Just want one thing
Just to play the king
But the castle's crumbled
And you're left with just a name

Where's your crown,
King Nothing?
Where's your crown?

Hot and cold, bought and sold
A heart as hard as gold
Are you satisfied?
Wish I might, wish I may
You wish your life away
Are you pacified?

All the wants you waste
All the things you've chased

Then it all crashes down
And you break your crown
And you point your finger
But there's no one around
Just want one thing
Just to play the king
But the castle's crumbled
And you're left with just a name

Where's your crown,
King Nothing?
Where's your crown?

I wish I may, I wish I might
Have this wish I wish tonight
I want that star, I want it now
I want it all and I don't care how

Careful what you wish
Careful what you say
Careful what you wish, you may
regret it
Careful what you wish, you just
might get it

Then it all crashes down
And you break your crown
And you point your finger
But there's no one around
Just want one thing
Just to play the king
But the castle's crumbled
And you're left with just a name

Where's your crown,
King Nothing?

Nothing

You're just nothing
Where's your crown,
King Nothing?
You're just nothing
Absolutely nothing

Off to never-never land

HERO OF THE DAY

Mama, they try and break me

The window burns to light the
  way back home
A light that warms no matter
  where they've gone
They're off to find the hero of
  the day
But what if they should fall by
  someone's wicked way?

Still the window burns
Time so slowly turns
And someone there is sighing
Keepers of the flames
Do you feel your name?
Did you hear your babies crying?

Mama, they try and break me
Still they try and break me

Excuse me while I tend to how
  I feel
These things return to me that
  still seem real
Now, deservingly, this easy chair
But the rocking stopped by
  wheels of despair

Don't want your aid
But the fist I make
For years can't hold or feel
No, I'm not all me
So please excuse me while I tend
  to how I feel

But now the dreams and
  waking screams
That ever last the night
So build the wall, behind it crawl
And hide until it's light
So can you hear your babies
  crying now?

Still the window burns
Time so slowly turns
And someone there is sighing
Keepers of the flames
Did you feel your names?
Did you hear your babies crying?

But now the dreams and
  waking screams
That ever last the night
So build a wall, behind it crawl
And hide until it's light
So can't you hear your babies
  crying now?

Mama, they try and break me
Mama, they try and break me
Mama they try
Mama they try

BLEEDING ME

I'm digging my way
I'm digging my way to
something
I'm digging my way to
something better

I'm pushing to stay
I'm pushing to stay with
something
I'm pushing to stay with
something better

I'm sowing the seeds
I'm sowing the seeds I've taken
I'm sowing the seeds I take
for granted

This thorn in my side
This thorn in my side is from
the tree
This thorn in my side is from the
tree I've planted

It tears me and I bleed
And I bleed

Caught under wheels' roll
I take the leech, I'm bleeding me
Can't stop to save my soul
I take the leash that's leading me
I'm bleeding me
I can't take it
Caught under wheels' roll
The bleeding of me
Of me
The bleeding of me

I am the beast that feeds
the feast
I am the blood, I am release

Come make me pure
Bleed me a cure
I'm caught, I'm caught, I'm
caught under

Caught under wheels' roll
I take that leech, I'm bleeding
me
Can't stop to save my soul
I take the leash that's leading me
I'm bleeding me
I can't take it
I can't take it
I can't take it
The bleeding of me

I'm digging my way
I'm digging my way to
something
I'm digging my way to
something better

I'm pushing to stay
I'm pushing to stay with
something
I'm pushing to stay with
something better
With something better

CURE

The man takes another bullet
He keeps them all within
He must seek no matter how
  it hurts
So don't fool again

He thinks the answer's cold
  and in his hand
He takes his medicine
The man takes another bullet
He's been fooled again

Uncross your arms
Take and throw them to the
  cure, say,
"I do believe"

Uncross your arms now
Take them to it, say
"I do believe"
"I do believe"

The lies tempt her and she
  follows
Again she lets him in
She must believe to fill the
  hollow
She's been fooled again

Uncross your arms
Take and throw them to
  the cure, say,
"I do believe"

Uncross your arms now
Take them to it, say,
"I do believe"
"Yeah, I do believe"

Betting on the cure
It must get better than this
Betting on the cure
Everyone's got to have the
  sickness
'Cause everyone seems to need
  the cure
Precious cure

Betting on the cure
'Cause it must get better than
  this
Betting on the cure
Everyone's got to have the
  sickness
'Cause everyone seems to need
  the cure
Precious cure

"I do believe"

Betting on the cure
It must get better than this
Need to feel secure
It's got to get better than this
It must get better than this
Betting on the cure
Everyone's got to have the
  sickness
'Cause everyone seems to
  need the cure

"I do believe"

POOR TWISTED ME

Oh, poor twisted me
Oh, poor twisted me
I feast on sympathy
I chew on suffer
I chew on agony

Swallow whole the pain
Oh, it's too good to be
That all this misery
Is just for, oh, poor twisted me
Poor twisted me

Poor mistreated me
Poor mistreated me
I drown without a sea
Lungs fill with sorrow
Lungs fill with misery

Inhaling the deep, dark blue
Oh, woe is me
Such a burden to be
The poor mistreated me

To finally reach the shore, survive the storm
Now you're bare and cold, the sea was warm
So warm, you bathe your soul again

Baby, again and again and again

You finally reached the shore, survived the storm
Now you're bare and cold, the sea was warm
So warm, you bathe your soul again

Good to feel my friend
Oh, woe is me
Such a burden to be
Oh, poor twisted me
Yo, poor twisted me

WASTING MY HATE

Good day. How do?
And I send a smile to you
Don't waste, waste your breath
And I won't waste my hate
  on you

Ain't gonna waste my hate
Ain't gonna waste my hate
  on you
I think I'll keep it for myself

Ain't gonna give no more
Ain't got the time to help
  you score
I think it's time you pleased
  yourself
Yourself

Good day. How do?
And I send a smile to you
Don't waste, waste your breath
And I won't waste my hate
  on you
Waste my hate on you
Hate

You think you're worthy now?
You think enough to even raise
  the brow
And to laugh and tip that
  two-pronged crown?

Well I see my hands, I see
  my feet
I feel that blood that pumps
  in beat
But where the hell's my mind
  going now?
Dead gone now

Good day. How do?
And I send a smile to you
Don't waste, waste your breath
And I won't waste my hate
  on you
Waste my hate on you

Think I'll keep it for myself

Hate

Ain't gonna waste my hate
But I'm so greedy when they say
Better to give than to receive

Ain't gonna waste my hate
Ain't got time to waste my
  hate on you
I think I'll keep it all for myself
For myself

Good day. How do?
And I send a smile to you
Don't waste, waste your breath
And I won't waste my hate
  on you
Waste my hate on you

Think I'll keep it for myself

Hate

MAMA SAID

Mama, she has taught me well
Told me when I was young
Son, your life's an open book
Don't close it 'fore it's done
The brightest flame burns
  quickest
That's what I heard her say
A son's heart's owed to mother
But I must find my way

Let my heart go
Let your son grow
Mama, let my heart go
Or, let this heart be still

"Rebel," my new last name
Wild blood in my veins
Apron strings around my neck
The mark that still remains
I left home at an early age
Of what I heard was wrong
I never asked forgiveness
But what is said is done

Let my heart go
Let your son grow
Mama, let my heart go
Or let this heart be still

Never I ask of you
But never I gave
But you gave me your emptiness
I now take to my grave
Never I ask of you
But never I gave
But you gave me your emptiness
I now take to my grave
So let this heart be still

Mama, now I'm coming home
I'm not all you wished of me
A mother's love for her son
Unspoken, help me be
I took your love for granted
And all the things you said
  to me
I need your arms to welcome me
But a cold stone's all I see

Let my heart go
Let your son grow
Mama, let my heart go
Or let this heart be still

Let my heart go
Mama, let my heart go
You never let my heart go
So let this heart be still

Never I ask of you
But never I gave
But you gave me your emptiness
I now take to my grave
Never I ask of you
But never I gave
But you gave me your emptiness
I now take to my grave
So let this heart be still

THE THORN WITHIN

Forgive me, Father, for I have sinned
Find me guilty of the life I feel within

When I'm branded, this mark of shame
Should I look down, disgraced, or straight ahead and know that you must blame?

I am the secret
I am the sin
I am the guilty
And I am, I am the thorn within

Forgive me, Father, for I have sinned
Find me guilty when true guilt is from within

So point your fingers, point right at me
For I am shadows and will follow you, one and the same are we

I am the secret
I am the sin
I am the guilty
And I am, I am the thorn within

I do your time, I take your fall
I'm branded guilty for us all

So point your fingers, point right at me
For I am shadows and will follow you, one and the same are we

I am your secrets
I am your sin
I am your guilty
And I am, I am the thorn within

I am the thorn within
I am the thorn within

RONNIE

Story starts, quiet town
Small-town boy, big-time frown
Never talks, never plays
Different path, lost his way

Then streets of red—red, I'm afraid—
There's no confetti, no parade
Nothing happens in this boring place
But, oh my God, how it all did change

Now they all pray,
"Blood stain, wash away"

He said,
"Lost my way
This bloody day
Lost my way"

I heard it
He said,
"Lost my way
This bloody day
Lost my way"
Oh, please wash away
But blood stained the sun red today

I always said something's wrong
With little, strange Ronnie Long
Never laughed, never smiled
Talked alone for miles and miles and miles

"Gallow calls, son," I say
Keep your smile and laugh all day
Think once again in this boring place
For little boys, how they soon change
And they all pray,
"Blood stain, wash away"

He said,
"I lost my way
This bloody day
Lost my way"

I heard it
He said,
"I lost my way
This bloody day
I lost my way"
Oh, please wash away
But blood stained the sun red today

Well, all the green things died when Ronnie moved to this place
He said, "Don't you dare ask why I'm cursed to wear this face"
Now we all know why the children called him Ronnie Frown
When he pulled that gun from his pocket they all fall down, down, down

He said,
"Lost my way
This bloody day
Lost my way"

Yeah, yeah
I heard it
He screamed,
"Lost my way
This bloody day
Lost my way"

Oh, please wash away
But blood stained the sun red today

All things wash away
And they all fall down
But blood stained the sun today

All things wash away
And they all fall down
But blood stained the sun today

THE OUTLAW TORN

And now I wait my whole
lifetime for you
And now I wait my whole
lifetime for you

I ride the dirt, I ride the tide for
you
I search the outside, search
inside for you

To take back what you left me
I know I'll always burn to be
The one who seeks so I may find
And now I wait my whole
lifetime

Outlaw of torn
Outlaw of torn
And I'm torn

So on I wait my whole lifetime
for you
So on I wait my whole lifetime
for you

The more I search, the more my
need for you
The more I bless, the more I
bleed for you

You make me smash the clock
and feel
I'd rather die behind the wheel
Time was never on my side
So on I wait my whole lifetime
Outlaw of torn
Outlaw of torn
Outlaw of torn
And I'm torn

Hear me
And if I close my mind in fear
Please pry it open
See me
And if my face becomes sincere
Beware
Hold me
And when I start to come
undone
Stitch me together
Save me
And when you see me strut
Remind me of what left this
outlaw torn

ReLoad

FUEL

Gimme fuel, gimme fire
Gimme that which I desire

Turn on, I see red
Adrenaline crash and crack
  my head
Nitro junkie, paint me dead
And I see red

One hundred plus through black
  and white
War horse, warhead
Fuck 'em, man, white-knuckle
  tight
Through black and white

On I burn
Fuel is pumping engines
Burning hard, loose and clean
And on I burn
Churning my direction
Quench my thirst with gasoline

So gimme fuel, gimme fire
Gimme that which I desire

Turn on beyond the bone
Swallow future, spit out home
Burn your face upon the chrome

Take the corner, join the crash,
Headlights, head on, headlines
Another junkie lives too fast
Lives way too fast

On I burn
Fuel is pumping engines
Burning hard, loose and clean
And on I burn
Churning my direction
Quench my thirst with gasoline

So gimme fuel, gimme fire
Gimme that which I desire

White-knuckle tight

Gimme fuel
Gimme fire
My desire

On I burn
Fuel is pumping engines
Burning hard, loose and clean
And on I burn
Churning my direction
Quench my thirst with gasoline

Gimme fuel, gimme fire
Gimme that which I desire

On I burn

THE MEMORY REMAINS

Fortune, fame
Mirror vain
Gone insane
But the memory remains

Heavy rings on fingers wave
Another star denies the grave
See the nowhere crowd cry the
  nowhere cheers of honor

Like twisted vines that grow
Hide and swallow mansions
  whole
And dim the light of an already
  faded prima donna

Fortune, fame
Mirror vain
Gone insane
Fortune, fame
Mirror vain
Gone insane
But the memory remains

Heavy rings hold cigarettes
Up to lips that time forgets
While the Hollywood sun sets
  behind your back

And can't the band play on?
Just listen, they play my song
Ash to ash, dust to dust,
  fade to black

Fortune, fame
Mirror vain
Gone insane
Fortune, fame
Mirror vain
Gone insane
Dance, little tin goddess

Drift away
Fade away
Little tin goddess

Ash to ash
Dust to dust
Fade to black

Fortune, fame
Mirror vain
Gone insane
Fortune, fame
Mirror vain
Gone insane
But the memory remains

Ash to ash
Dust to dust
Fade to black
But the memory remains

To this faded prima donna

Dance, little tin goddess, dance

DEVIL'S DANCE

I feel you too
Feel those things you do
In your eyes I see a fire
  that burns
To free the you
That's wanting through
Deep inside you know the
  seeds I plant will grow

One day you will see
And dare to come down to me
C'mon, c'mon now take
  the chance
That's right, let's dance

Snake, I am the snake
Tempting, that bite to take
Let me make your mind
Leave yourself behind
Be not afraid
I've got what you need
Hunger I will feed

One day you will see
And dare to come down to me
C'mon, c'mon now take
  the chance
Come dance

One day you will see
And dare to come down to me
C'mon, c'mon now take
  the chance

I feel you too
Feel those things you do
In your eyes I see a fire
  that burns
To free the you
That's running through
Deep inside you know
Seeds I plant will grow

One day you will see
And dare to come down to me
C'mon, c'mon now take
  the chance
That's right
Let's dance

It's nice to see you here

THE UNFORGIVEN II

Lay beside me, tell me what they've done
Speak the words I want to hear, to make my demons run
The door is locked now but it's opened if you're true
If you can understand the me, then I can understand the you

Lay beside me, under wicked skies
Through black of day, dark of night, we share this paralyze
The door cracks open but there's no sun shining through
Black heart scarring darker still, but there's no sun shining through

No, there's no sun shining through
No, there's no sun shining

What I've felt, what I've known
Turn the pages, turn the stone
Behind the door, should I open it for you?

What I've felt, what I've known
Sick and tired, I stand alone
Could you be there, 'cause I'm the one who waits for you
Or are you unforgiven, too?

Come beside me, this won't hurt, I swear
She loves me not, she loves me still, but she'll never love again
She lay beside me but she'll be there when I'm gone
Black heart scarring darker still, yes, she'll be there when I'm gone
Yes, she'll be there when I'm gone
Dead sure she'll be there

What I've felt, what I've known
Turn the pages, turn to stone
Behind the door, should I open it for you?

What I've felt, what I've known
Sick and tired, I stand alone
Could you be there, 'cause I'm the one who waits for you
Or are you unforgiven, too?

Lay beside me, tell me what I've done
The door is closed, so are your eyes
But now I see the sun, now I see the sun
Yes, now I see it

What I've felt, what I've known
Turn the pages, turn the stone
Behind the door, should I open it for you?

What I've felt, what I've known
Sick and tired, I stand alone
Could you be there? 'Cause I'm the one who waits
The one who waits for you

I take this key
And I bury it in you
Because you're unforgiven, too

Never free
Never me
'Cause you're unforgiven, too

BETTER THAN YOU

I look at you, then you, me
Hungry and thirsty are we
Holding the lion's share, holding the key
Holding me back 'cause I'm striving to be

Better than you
Better than you

Lock horns, I push and I strive
Somehow I feel more alive
Bury the need for it, bury the seed
Bury me deep when there's no will to be

Better than you
Better than you

Can't stop this train from rolling
Nothing brings me down
No, can't stop this train from rolling on and on, on
Forever on and on

Can't stop this train from rolling
You can't take it down
No, never stop this locomotion, on and on and on
No, you can't bring me down 'cause I'm

Better than you
Better than you

SLITHER

Don't go looking for snakes,
  you might find them
Don't send your eyes to the sun,
  you might blind them
Haven't I seen you here before?

Watch the puppets dancing
See the clowns fall down
Tie your tap shoes tightly
And wear them into town

See you crawlin'
See you crawlin' in

Don't go looking for snakes,
  you might find them
Don't send your eyes to the sun,
  you might blind them
Haven't I seen you here before?
There ain't no heroes here, no,
  no more

Play the game so nicely
Check, it's your move now
We're standing in this jungle
With serpents I have found

See you crawlin'
See you crawlin' in

Don't go looking for snakes,
  you might find them
Don't send your eyes to the sun,
  you might blind them
Haven't I seen you here before?
Have your heroes disappeared?

See you crawlin'
See you crawlin' in

So don't go looking for snakes,
  you might find them
Don't send your eyes to the sun,
  you might blind them
Haven't I seen you here before?
No, there ain't no heroes here,
  no

Haven't I seen you here before?
No there ain't no heroes here

Don't go looking for snakes,
  you might find them
Haven't I seen you here before?
Have your heroes disappeared?
Don't send your eyes to the sun,
  you might blind them

CARPE DIEM BABY

Hit dirt
Shake tree
Split sky
Part sea

Strip smile
Lose cool
Bleed the day
And break the rule

Live, win
Dare, fail
Eat the dirt
And bite the nail

Then make me miss you
Then make me miss you

So wash your face away
  with dirt
It don't feel good until it hurts
So take this world and shake it
Come squeeze and suck the day
Come carpe diem, baby

Draw lead
Piss wine
Sink teeth
All mine

Stoke fire
Break neck
Suffer through this
Cheat on death

Hug the curve
Lose the time
Tear the map
And shoot the sign

Then make me miss you
Then make me miss you

So wash your face away
  with dirt
It don't feel good until it hurts
So take this world and shake it
Come squeeze and suck the day
Come carpe diem, baby

Live, win
Dare, fail
Eat dirt
Bite the nail

Strip smile
Lose cool
Bleed the day
And break the rule

Hug the curve
Lose the time
Tear the map
And shoot the sign

Then make me miss you
Then make me miss you

So wash your face away
  with dirt
It don't feel good until it hurts
So take this world and shake it
Come squeeze and suck the day

Come make me miss you
Come carpe diem, baby
Come carpe diem, baby

BAD SEED

Come clean, fess up
Tell all, spill gut
Off the veil, stand revealed
Show the cards, bring it on,
break the seal

Ladies and gentlemen,
step right up
And see the man who told
the truth

Swing the noose again
Pierce the apple skin
You bit more than you need
Now you're choking on
the bad seed
On the bad seed
Choking

Let on, load off
Confess, cast off
At the mercy, the cat is out
Drop the disguise, spit it up,
spit it out

And now, what you've all
been waiting for
I give you He Who Suffers
the Truth

Swing the noose again
Pierce the apple skin
You bit more than you need
Now you're choking on the
bad seed
Choking on the bad seed

Off the veil, stand revealed
Bring it on, break the seal
At the mercy, cat is out
Spit it up, spit it out
Spit it up, spit it out
Spit it out now

At the mercy

Swing the noose again
Pierce the apple skin
You bit more than you need
Choking on the seed

Swing the noose again
Pierce the apple skin
You bit more than you need
You're choking on the bad seed

Off the veil, stand revealed
Bring it on, break the seal
At the mercy, cat is out
Spit it up, spit it out
Spit it up, spit it out
Spit it out now

Choking on the bad seed

WHERE THE WILD THINGS ARE

So wake up, sleepy one
It's time to save your world

Steal dreams and give to you
Shoplift a thought or two
All children touch the sun
Burn fingers one by one, by one

Will this earth be good to you?
Keep you clean or stain through?

So wake up, sleepy one
It's time to save your world
You're where the wild things are
Toy soldiers off to war

Big eyes to open soon
Believing all under sun and
  moon
But does heaven know
  you're here?
And did they give you smiles
  or tears?
No, no tears

Will this earth be good to you?
Keep you clean or stain through?

So wake up, sleepy one
It's time to save your world
You're where the wild things are
Toy soldiers off to war

You swing your rattle down
Call to arms, the trumpets sound
Toy horses start the charge
Robot chessmen standing guard
Hand puppets storm the beach
Fire trucks trapped out of reach
Hand puppets storm the beach
Fire trucks trapped out of reach
All clowns reinforce the rear
Slingshots fire into the air
All clowns reinforce the rear
Slingshots fire into the air
Stuffed bears hold the hill
  till death
Crossfire from the marionettes
Stuffed bears hold the hill
  till death
Crossfire from the marionettes
We shall never surrender

All you children touch the sun
Burn your fingers one by one
Will this earth be good to you?
Keep you clean or stain through?

So wake up, sleepy one
It's time to save your world
You're where the wild things are
Toy soldiers off to war
Off to war
Off to war

So close your little eyes

PRINCE CHARMING

There's a black cloud overhead
That's me
And the poison ivy chokes the tree
Again it's me
I'm the filthy one on Bourbon Street you walk on by
I'm the little boy that pushes hard and makes it cry

There's a dirty needle in your child
Stick me
Empty bottles still in hand, still dead
Still me
I'm the suit and tie that bleeds the street and still wants more
I'm the forty-five that's in your mouth, I'm a dirty, dirty whore

Look, it's me
The one who can't be free
Much too young to focus
But too old to see

Hey, look, it's me
What no one wants to see
See what you brought this world
Just what you want to see
Hey, Ma
Hey, Mom! Look, it's me

And he wants to be called "Father" now
Me again, me
The marks inside your arms spell me
Spell only me
I'm the nothing face that plants the bomb and strolls away
I'm the one who doesn't look quite right as children play

Look, it's me
The one who can't be free
Much too young to focus
But too old to see

Hey, look, it's me
What no one wants to see
See what you brought this world
Just what you want you want to see
Hey, Ma
Hey, Ma! Look, it's me

Look up to me,
What to be and what to fear
Look up to me
Look, it's me. Like what you hear?
See right through me
See the one who can't be free
See right through me
Look, it's me, what no one wants to see

Now see the black cloud up ahead
That's me
And this poison ivy chokes the tree
Again it's me
And I'm the filthy one on Bourbon Street you walk on by
I'm the little boy that pushes, pushes, makes it cry

Look, it's me
The one who can't be free
Much too young to focus
But too old to see

Hey, look, it's me
What no one wants to see
See what you brought this world
Just what you want to see
Hey, Ma
Hey, Ma! Look, it's me

Hey, Ma
Hey, Ma! Look, it's me

LOW MAN'S LYRIC

My eyes seek reality
My fingers seek my veins
There's a dog at your back step
He must come in from the rain

I fall 'cause I've let go
The net below has rot away
So my eyes seek reality
And my fingers seek my veins

The trash fire is warm
But nowhere safe from the
storm
And I can't bear to see
What I've let me be
So wicked and worn

So as I write to you
Of what is done and to do
Maybe you'll understand
And you won't cry for this man
'Cause low man is due

Please forgive me

My eyes seek reality
My fingers feel for faith
Touch clean with a dirty hand
I touch the clean to the waste

The trash fire is warm
But nowhere safe from the storm
And I can't bear to see
What I've let me be
So wicked and worn

So as I write to you
Of what is done and to do
Maybe you'll understand
And won't cry for this man
'Cause low man is due

Please forgive me

So low, the sky is all I see
All I want from you is forgive me
So you bring this poor dog in
from the rain
Though he just wants right back
out again

And I cry to the alleyway
Confess all to the rain
But I lie, lie straight to the mirror
The one I've broken to match
my face

The trash fire is warm
But nowhere safe from the
storm
And I can't bear to see
What I've let me be
So wicked and worn

So as I write to you
Of what is done and to do
Maybe you'll understand
And won't cry for this man
'Cause low man is due

Please forgive me

So low, the sky is all I see
All I want from you is forgive me
So you bring this poor dog in
from the rain
Though he just wants right back
out again

My eyes seek reality
My fingers seek my veins

ATTITUDE

Suppose I say "I'm never satisfied"
Suppose I say "You cut some
root to make the tree survive"

Just let me kill you for a while
Just let me kill you for a smile
Just let me kill you once
I'm oh so bored to death

I hunger
I hunger
I eat

Born into attitude
Asleep at the wheel
Throw all your bullets in the fire
And run like hell
Why cure the fever?
Whatever happened to sweat?

Suppose I say "The vultures
smile at me"
Suppose I say "I've sent them
down and they plan to pick
you clean"

And satisfaction this way comes
And satisfaction this way comes
And satisfaction's here and
gone, gone
Gone again

I hunger
I hunger
I eat

Born into attitude
Asleep at the wheel
Throw all your bullets in the fire
And stand there

Born into attitude
Twist mother tongue
Throw all your bullets in the fire
And run like hell
Why cure the fever?
Whatever happened to sweat?

Just let me kill you for a while
Just let me kill you for a smile
Just let me kill you once for me
I'm bored to death

And satisfaction this way comes
And satisfaction this way comes
And satisfaction's here and
gone, gone
Gone again

I hunger
I hunger
I eat

Born into attitude
Asleep at the wheel
Throw all your bullets in the fire
And stand there

Born into attitude
Twist mother tongue
Throwing all your bullets in
the fire
And run like hell
Why cure the fever?
Whatever happened to sweat?

FIXXXER

Dolls of voodoo all stuck with pins
One for each of us and our sins
So you lay us in a line
Push your pins, they make us humble
Only you can tell in time
If we fall or merely stumble

But tell me, can you heal what Father's done?
Or fix this hole in a mother's son?
Can you heal the broken worlds within?
Can you strip away so we may start again?

Tell me, can you heal what Father's done?
Or cut this rope and let us run?
Just when all seems fine and I'm pain free
You jab another pin, jab another pin in me

Mirror, mirror, upon thy wall
Break the spell or become the doll
See you sharpening the pins
So the holes will remind us
We're just the toys in the hands of another
And in time the needles turn from shine to rust

But tell me, can you heal what Father's done?
Or fix this hole in a mother's son?
Can you heal the broken worlds within?
Can you strip away so we may start again?

Tell me, can you heal what Father's done?
Or cut this rope and let us run?
Just when all seems fine and I'm pain free
You jab another pin, jab another pin in me

Blood for face, sweat for dirt
Three Xs for the stone
To break this curse a ritual's due
I believe I'm not alone
Shell of shotgun, pint of gin
Numb us up to shield the pins
Renew our faith, which way we can
To fall in love with life again
To fall in love with life again
To fall in love with life again
To fall in love
To fall in love
To fall in love with life again

So tell me, can you heal what Father's done?
Or fix this hole in a mother's son?
Can you heal the broken worlds within?
Can you strip away so we may start again?

Tell me, can you heal what Father's done?
Or cut this rope and let us run?
Just when all seems fine and I'm pain free
You jab another pin, jab another pin in me

No more pins in me
No more, no more pins in me

S & M

NO LEAF CLOVER

And it feels right this time
On his crash course with the big time
Pay no mind to the distant thunder
New day fills his head with wonder, boy

Says it feels right this time
Turned it 'round and found the right line
"Good day to be alive, sir
Good day to be alive," he says

Then it comes to be that the soothing light at the end of your tunnel
Was just a freight train coming your way
Then it comes to be that the soothing light at the end of your tunnel
Was just a freight train coming your way

Don't it feel right like this?
All the pieces fall to his wish
"Sucker for that quick reward, boy
Sucker for that quick reward," they say

Then it comes to be that the soothing light at the end of your tunnel
Was just a freight train coming your way
Then it comes to be that the soothing light at the end of your tunnel
Was just a freight train coming your way
It's coming your way

Then it comes to be that the soothing light at the end of your tunnel
Was just a freight train coming your way

Then it comes to be
Then it comes to be

– HUMAN

Don't you leave me, Father Time
Take me with you
Tell me, does your sun still shine?
Come squeeze the world and drip it down my throat again
Down my throat again

You got to breathe, man, breathe
Coming up for air
Breathe, man, breathe
Coming up for air

Touch me so I think I'm here
Skin my senses
Barely breathing, minus human
Just squeeze the world and drip it down my throat again
Down my throat again

You got to breathe, man, breathe
Coming up for air
Breathe, man, breathe
Coming up for air

MISSION: IMPOSSIBLE 2
(SOUNDTRACK)

I DISAPPEAR

Here I go now
Here I go into new days
Here I go now
Here I go into new days
I'm pain, I'm hope, I'm suffer
Here I go into new days

Ain't no mercy
Ain't no mercy there for me
Ain't no mercy
Ain't no mercy there for me
I'm pain, I'm hope, I'm suffer
Ain't no mercy
Ain't no mercy there for me

Do you bury me when I'm gone?
Do you teach me while I'm here?
Just as soon as I belong
Then it's time I disappear

And I went
And I went on down that road
And I went on
And I went on down that road
I'm pain, I'm hope, I'm suffer
And I went on
And I went on down that road

Do you bury me when I'm gone?
Do you teach me while I'm here?
Just as soon as I belong
Then it's time I disappear

st. Anger

FRANTIC

If I could have my wasted days
back
Would I use them to get back
on track?
Stop to warm at karma's burning
Or look ahead, but keep on
turning?

Do I have the strength
To know how I'll go?
Can I find it inside
To deal with what I shouldn't
know?

Could I have my wasted days
back
Would I use them to get back
on track?

You live it or lie it!

My lifestyle determines my
deathstyle

Keep searching, keep on
searching
This search goes on, this search
goes on

Frantic Tick Tick Tick Tick Tick
Tock
Frantic Tick Tick Tick Tick Tick
Tock

I've worn out always being afraid
An endless stream of fear that
I've made
Treading water full of worry
This frantic tick tick talk of hurry

Do I have the strength
To know how I'll go?
Can I find it inside
To deal with what I shouldn't
know?

Worn out always being afraid
An endless stream of fear that
I've made

You live it or lie it!

My lifestyle determines my
deathstyle

Keep searching, keep on
searching
This search goes on, this search
goes on

Frantic Tick Tick Tick Tick Tick
Tock
Frantic Tick Tick Tick Tick Tick
Tock

My lifestyle (Birth is pain)
Determines my deathstyle
(Life is pain)
A rising tide (Death is pain)
That pushes to the other side
(It's all the same)

ST. ANGER

Saint Anger 'round my neck
Saint Anger 'round my neck
He never gets respect
Saint Anger 'round my neck

You flush it out, you flush it out
Saint Anger 'round my neck
You flush it out, you flush it out
He never gets respect

Fuck it all and no regrets
I hit the lights on these dark sets
I need a voice to let myself
To let myself go free
Fuck it all and fuckin' no regrets
I hit the lights on these dark sets
Medallion noose, I hang myself
Saint Anger 'round my neck

I feel my world shake
Like an earth quake
It's hard to see clear
Is it me? Is it fear?

I'm madly in anger with you

And I want my anger to be healthy
And I want my anger just for me
And I need my anger not to control
And I want my anger to be me

And I need to set my anger free

Set it free

SOME KIND OF MONSTER

These are the eyes that can't see me
These are the hands that drop your trust
These are the boots that kick you around
This is the tongue that speaks on the inside
These are the ears that ring with hate
This is the face that'll never change
This is the fist that grinds you down
This is the voice of silence no more

These are the legs in circles run
This is the beating you'll never know
These are the lips that taste no freedom
This is the feel that's not so safe
This is the face you'll never change
This is the god that ain't so pure
This is the god that is not pure
This is the voice of silence no more

We the people
Are we the people?

Some kind of monster
The monster lives

This is the face that stones you cold
This is the moment that needs to breathe
These are the claws that scratch these wounds
This is the pain that never leaves
This is the tongue that whips you down
This is the burden of every man
These are the screams that pierce your skin
This is the voice of silence no more

This is the test of flesh and soul
This is the trap that smells so good
This is the flood that drains these eyes
These are the looks that chill to the bone
These are the fears that swing over head
These are the weights that hold you down
This is the end that will never end
This is the voice of silence no more

We the people
Are we the people?

Some kind of monster
The monster lives

This is the cloud that swallows trust
This is the black that uncolors us
This is the face that you hide from
This is the mask that comes undone

Ominous
I'm in us

DIRTY WINDOW

I see my reflection in the
window
It looks different, so different
than what you see
Projecting judgment on the
world
This house is clean baby
This house is clean

Am I who I think I am?
Am I who I think I am?
Am I who I think I am?
Well, look out my window and
see it's gone wrong
Court is in session and I slam my
gavel down

I'm judge and I'm jury and I'm
executioner too

Projector
Protector
Rejector
Infector
Projector
Rejector
Infector
Injector
Defector
Rejector

I see my reflection in the
window
This window clean inside, dirty
on the out
I'm looking different than me
This house is clean baby
This house is clean

Am I who I think I am?
Am I who I think I am?
Am I who I think I am?
Well, I look out my window and
see it's gone wrong
But court is in session and now I
slam my gavel down

Projector
Protector
Rejector
Infector
Projector
Rejector
Infector
Injector
Defector
Rejector
Defector

I drink from the cup of denial
I'm judging the world from my
throne
I drink from the cup of denial
I'm judging the world from my
throne

INVISIBLE KID

Invisible kid
Never see what he did
Got stuck where he hid
Fallen through the grid

Invisible kid
Got a place of his own
Where he'll never be known
Inward he's grown

Invisible kid
Locked away in his brain
From the shame and the pain
World down the drain

Invisible kid
Suspicious of your touch
Don't want no crutch
But it's all too much

I hide inside
I hurt inside
I hide inside, but I'll show you…

I'm OK, just go away
Into the distance let me fade
I'm OK, just go away
I'm OK, but please don't stray
too far

Open up your heart
I'm beating right here
Open your mind
I'm being right here, right now
Open your heart
I'm beating right here
Open your mind
I'm being right here, right now

Ooh, what a good boy you are
Out of the way and you're kept
to yourself
Ooh, can't you see that he's
not here
He doesn't want the attention
you give
Ooh, unplugging from it all
Invisible kid floats alone in
his room
Ooh, what a quiet boy you are
He looks so calm floating 'round
and 'round in himself

MY WORLD

The motherfuckers got in my
head
Trying to make me someone
else instead

It's my world now

Mama, why's it rainin' in my
room?
Cheer up boy, clouds will move
on soon
Heavy fog got me lost inside
I'm gonna sit right back and
enjoy this ride

It's my world
You can't have it
It's my world, it's my world
It's my world
Sucker!

I'm out of my head, out of my
head
Get 'em out of my head, out of
my head
Get 'em out

Who's in charge of my head
today?
Dancin' devils in angels way

It's my time now

Look out motherfuckers here I
come
I'm gonna make my head my
home
The sons of bitches tryin' to take
my head
Tryin' to make me someone else
instead

It's my world
You can't have it
It's my world, it's my world
It's my world

Yeah, I'm out of my head, out of
my head
Get 'em out of my head, out of
my head
Get 'em out

Not only do I not know the
answer
I don't even know what the
question is

God it feels like it only rains
on me

Not only do I not know the
answer
I don't even know what the
question is
Sucker!

Out of my head, out of my head
Out of my head
Get 'em out of my head
Get 'em out!

Enough's enough

SHOOT ME AGAIN

I won't go away
Right here I'll stay

Stand silent in flames
Stand tall 'till it fades

Shoot me again
I ain't dead yet

Shoot me again

All the shots I take
I spit back at you
All the shit you fake
Comes back to haunt you

All the shots

All the shots I take
What difference did I make?
All the shots I take
I spit back at you

I won't go away, with a bullet in my back
Right here I'll stay, with a bullet in my back

Shoot me
Take a shot

I'll stand on my own, with a bullet in my back
I'm stranded and sold, with a bullet in my back

Yeah, I bite my tongue
Trying not to shoot back
No compromise
My heart won't pump the other way

Wake the sleeping giant
Wake the beast
Wake the sleeping dog
No, let him sleep

SWEET AMBER

Wash your back so you won't stab mine
Get in bed with your own kind
Live your life so you don't see mine
Drape your back so you won't shine

Ooh then she holds my hand
And I lie to get a smile

Using what I want
To get what you want

Ooh Sweet Amber
How sweet are you?
How sweet does it get?

Chase the rabbit, fetch the stick
She rolls me over 'till I'm sick
She deals in habits, deals in pain
I run away, but I'm back again

Mm then she holds my hand
And I lie to get a smile
Mm and she squeezes tighter
I still lie to get a smile

She holds the pen that spells the end
She traces me and draws me in
It's never as sweet as it seems

THE UNNAMED FEELING

Been here before

Been here before couldn't say I liked it
Yeah, do I start writing all this down?
Just let me plug you into my world
Can't you help me be uncrazy?

Name this for me, heat the cold air
Take the chill off of my life
And if I could I'd turn my eyes
To look inside to see what's coming

It comes alive
And I could die a little more
It comes alive
Each moment here I die a little more

Then the unnamed feeling
It comes alive
Then the unnamed feeling
Takes me away

I'm frantic in your soothing arms
I cannot sleep in this down filled world
I've found safety in this loneliness
But I cannot stand it anymore

Cross my heart, hope not to die
Swallow evil, ride the sky
Lose myself in a crowded room
You fool, you fool, it will be here soon

It comes alive
And I die a little more
It comes alive
Each moment here I die a little more

Then the unnamed feeling
It comes alive
Then the unnamed feeling
Treats me this way
And I wait for this train
Toes over the line
And then the unnamed feeling
Takes me away

Get the fuck out of here
I just wanna get the fuck away from me
I rage, I glaze, I hurt, I hate
I hate it all, why? Why? Why me?

I cannot sleep with a head like this
I wanna cry, I wanna scream
I rage, I glaze, I hurt, I hate
I wanna hate it all away

PURIFY

Tear it down
Strip the layers off
My turpentine
Old paint, old looks
Cover up the past
White heat, white light
Super white bones
Bones of you and I

Pure if I... Can't you help me?
Pure if I... Won't you help me?
Purify you and I
Purify you and I
Pure if I... Can't you help me?
Pure if I... Won't you help me?
You and I purify

Truth and dare
Peeling back the skin
Acid wash
Ghost white
Ultra clean
Wannabe skeleton
Clear eyes
Diamond eyes
Strip the past of mine
My sweet turpentine

I can find the dirt on anything
I can find the dirt on anything

I ain't dancing with your skeletons
I ain't dancing with what might have been

ALL WITHIN MY HANDS

All within my hands
Squeeze it in, crush it down
All within my hands
Hold it dear, hold it suffocate

All within my hands
Love to death, smack you 'round
& 'round and
All within my hands
Beware

Love is control
I'll die if I let go

Hate me now
Kill all within my hands
Hate me now
Crush all within my hands
Squeeze all within my hands
Choke all within my hands
Hate me now
Trap all within my hands
Hurry up and hate me now
Kill all within my hands again

All within my hands
Take your fear, pump me up
All within my hands
Let you run, then I pull your
leash

All within my hands
Under thumb, under to myself
All within my hands
Beware

Love is control
I'll die if I let go
Let it go

Hate me now
Kill all within my hands
Hate me now
Crush all within my hands
Squeeze all within my hands
Choke all within my hands
Hate me now
Trap all within my hands
Hurry up and hate me now
Kill all within my hands again

I'll die if I let go
Control is love, love is control
I'll fall if I let go
Control is love, love is control

I will only let you breathe
My air that you receive
Then we'll see if I let you love
me

Kill Kill Kill Kill Kill

DEATH MAGNETIC

THAT WAS JUST YOUR LIFE

Like a siren in my head that always threatens to repeat
Like a blind man that is strapped into the speeding drivers seat
Like a face
That learns to speak
When all it knew was how to bite

Like a misery that keeps me focused though I've gone astray
Like an endless nightmare that I must awaken from each day
Like conviction
A premonition
Not worthy of, so I deny...I deny

I blind my eyes and try to force it all into place
I stitch them up, see not my fall from grace
I blind my eyes, I hide and feel it passing me by
I open just in time to say goodbye

Almost like your life
Almost like your endless fight
Curse the day is long
Realize you don't belong
Disconnect somehow
Never stop the bleeding now

Almost like your fight
And there it went,
Almost like your life

Like a wound that keeps on bleeding to remind me not to think
Like a raging river drowning when I only need a drink
Like a poison
That I swallow
But I want the world to die

Like a release from a prison that I didn't know I was in
Like a fight to live the past I prayed to leave from way back then
Like a general
Without a mission
Until the war will start again...start again

I blind my eyes and try to force it all into place
I stitch them up, see not my fall from grace
I blind my eyes, I hide and feel it passing me by
I open just in time to say goodbye

Almost like your life
Almost like your endless fight
Curse the day is long
Realize you don't belong
Disconnect somehow
Never stop the bleeding now

Almost like your fight
And there it went,
Almost like your life

Like a touch from hell to feel how hot
That it can get if you get caught
Like a strike from heaven turns that key
And brings you straight down to your knees
Like a touch from hell to feel how hot
That it can get if I get caught
Like a strike from heaven to reprieve
That brings you straight down to your knees

Almost like your life
Almost like your endless fight
Curse the day is long
Realize you don't belong
Disconnect somehow
Never stop the bleeding now

Almost like your fight
And there it went,
Almost like your life

That was just your life

THE END OF THE LINE

Need...more and more
Tainted misery

Bleed...battle scars
Chemical affinity

Reign...legacy
Innocence corrode

Stain...rot away
Catatonic overload

Choke...asphyxia
Snuff reality

Scorch...kill the light
Incinerate celebrity

Reaper...butchery
Karma amputee

Bloodline...redefine
Death contagious deity

Hooked into this deceiver
Need more and more
Into the endless fever
Need more and more

New consequence machine
You burn through all your
gasoline.
Asylum overtime
Nevermind...
You've reached the end of the
line

Time...choke the clock
Steal another day

Die...faithfully
Narcissistic fade away

Twisted...jump the rail
Shatter the ground below

Breaker...chase the ghost
From latest high to all-time low

Hooked into this deceiver
Need more and more
Into the endless fever
Need more and more

New consequence machine
You burn through all your
gasoline
Asylum overtime
Nevermind...
You've reached the end of the
line

Drop the hourglass of time
Spilling sand we will not find
As we gather here today
We bid farewell...
The slave becomes the master
The slave becomes the master
The slave becomes the master

The slave becomes the master
Need more and more
Right now and ever after
Need more and more

New consequence machine
You burn through all your
gasoline
Asylum overtime
Nevermind...

Dead hourglass of time
Sand we will not ever find
We gather here today
Say goodbye
Cause you've reached the end of the line

The end of the line
The end of the line
The end of the line

You've reached the end of the line

BROKEN, BEAT & SCARRED

You rise, you fall
You're down, then you rise again
What don't kill ya make ya more strong
You rise, you fall
You're down, then you rise again
What don't kill ya make ya more strong

Rise, fall, down, rise again
What don't kill ya make ya more strong
Rise, fall, down, rise again
What don't kill ya make ya more strong

Through black days
Through black nights
Through pitch black insides

Breaking your teeth on the hard life comin'
Show your scars
Cutting your feet on the hard earth runnin'
Show your scars

Breaking your life, broken, beat and scarred
But we die hard

The dawn, the death
The fight to the final breath
What don't kill ya make ya more strong
The dawn, the death
The fight to the final breath
What don't kill ya make ya more strong

Dawn, death, fight, final breath
What don't kill ya make ya more strong
Dawn, death, fight, final breath
What don't kill ya make ya more strong

They scratch me
They scrape me
They cut and rape me

Breaking your teeth on the hard life comin'
Show your scars
Cutting your feet on the hard earth runnin'
Show your scars

Breaking your life, broken, beat and scarred
(But) we die hard

Breaking your teeth on the hard life comin'
Show your scars
Cutting your feet on the hard earth runnin'
Show your scars

Bleeding your soul in a hard luck story
Show your scars
Spilling your blood in the hot sun's glory
Show your scars

Breaking your life, broken, beat and scarred
(But) we die hard
We die hard
We die hard

THE DAY THAT NEVER COMES

Born to push you around
Better just stay down
You pull away
He hits the flesh
You hit the ground

Mouth so full of lies
Tend to black your eyes
Just keep them closed
Just keep praying
Just keep waiting

Waiting for the one
The day that never comes
When you stand up and feel the
warmth
But the son shine never comes
No, the son shine never comes

Push you cross that line,
Just stay down this time
Hide in yourself
Crawl in yourself
You'll have your time

God I'll make them pay
Take it back one day
I'll end this day
I'll splatter color on this gray

Waiting for the one
The day that never comes
When you stand up and feel the
warmth
But the son shine never comes

Love... is a four letter word
And never spoken here
Love... is a four letter word
Here in this prison
I suffer this no longer
I'll put an end to this, I swear

This, I swear
The son will shine

This, I swear
This, I swear
This, I swear!

ALL NIGHTMARE LONG

Luck. Runs. Out.
Crawl from the wreckage one more time
Horrific memory twists the mind
Dark, rutted, cold and hard to turn
Path of destruction feel it burn

Still life… incarnation
Still life… infamy
Hallucination
Heresy
Still you run, what's to come, what's to be?

Cause we...
Hunt you down without mercy
Hunt you down all nightmare long
Feel us breathe upon your face
Feel us shift, every move we trace
Hunt you down without mercy
Hunt you down all nightmare long
Luck. Runs. Out.
You crawl back in, but your luck runs out

Luck. Runs. Out.
The light that is not light is here
To flush you out with your own fear
You hide, you hide but will be found
Release your grip without a sound

Still life… immolation
Still life… infamy
Hallucination
Heresy
Still you run, what's to come, what's to be?

Cause we...
Hunt you down without mercy
Hunt you down all nightmare long
Feel us breathe upon your face
Feel us shift, every move we trace
Hunt you down without mercy
Hunt you down all nightmare long
Luck. Runs. Out.
You crawl back in, but your luck runs out

Then you crawl back in
Into your obsession
Never to return
This is your confession

Cause we…
Hunt you down without mercy
Hunt you down all nightmare long
Feel us breathe upon your face
Feel us shift, every move we trace
Hunt you down without mercy
Hunt you down all nightmare long
Luck. Runs. Out.
You crawl back in, but your luck runs out

Your luck runs out

CYANIDE

Sleep and dream of this
Death angels kiss
Brings final bliss
Completely

Empty they say
Death, won't you let me stay?
Empty they say
Death, hear me call your name
call your name...

...SUICIDE
I've already died
You're just the funeral I've been
waiting for

...CYANIDE
Living dead inside
Break this empty shell for ever
more

Wait, wait patiently
Your death black wings
unfolding sleep
Spreading o'er me

Empty they say
Death, won't you let me stay?
Empty they say
Death, hear me call your name
call your name...

...SUICIDE
I've already died
You're just the funeral I've been
waiting for

...CYANIDE
Living dead inside
Break this empty shell for ever
more

Say, is that rain or are they
tears?
That has stained your concrete
face for years
The crying, weeping, shedding
strife
Year after year, life after life

An air of freshly broken ground
A concrete angel lit right down
upon the grave which swallows
fast
It's peace at last, Oh peace at
last!

Empty they say
Death, won't you let me stay?
Empty they say
Death, hear me call your name,
call your name...

...SUICIDE
I've already died
You're just the funeral I've been
waiting for

...CYANIDE
Living dead inside
Break this empty shell for ever
more

To win this war
Forever more
You're just the funeral I've been
waiting for

THE UNFORGIVEN III

How could he know this new
dawn's light
Would change his life forever?
Set sail to sea, but pulled off
course
By the light of golden treasure

Was he the one causing pain
With his careless dreaming?
Been afraid, always afraid
Of the things he's feeling

He could just be gone
He would just sail on
He'll just sail on

How can I be lost, if I've got
nowhere to go?
Search for seas of gold, how
come it's got so cold?
How can I be lost? In remem-
brance I relive
And how can I blame you, when
it's me I can't forgive?

These days drift on inside a fog
It's thick and suffocating
His sinking life, outside its hell
Inside, intoxicating

He's run aground. Like his life
Water much too shallow
Slipping fast, down with his ship
Fading in the shadows

Now a castaway
They've all gone away
They've gone away

How can I be lost, if I've got
nowhere to go?
Search for seas of gold, how
come it's got so cold?
How can I be lost, in remem-
brance I relive?
And how can I blame you, when
it's me I can't forgive?

Forgive me
Forgive me not

Why can't I forgive me?

Set sail to sea, but pulled off
course
By the light of golden treasure
How could he know this new
dawn's light
Would change his life forever?
How can I be lost, if I've got
nowhere to go?
Search for seas of gold, how
come it's got so cold?
How can I be lost? In remem-
brance I relive
So how can I blame you, when
it's me I can't forgive?

THE JUDAS KISS

When the world has turned its
back
When the days have turned pitch
black

When the fear abducts your
tongue
When the fire's dead and gone

So, What now?
Where go I?
When you think it's all said and
done

When you are the ostracized
Selfish ridden dead goodbye

Twisting on the tourniquet
When the pieces never fit

So, What now?
Where go I?
When you think it's all said and
done

Bow down
Sell your soul to me
I will set you free
Pacify your demons
Bow down
Surrender unto me
Submit infectiously
Sanctify your demons

Into abyss
You don't exist
Cannot resist
The Judas kiss

When the storm has blacked
your sky
Institution crucify

When the ego strips your reign
Assassinate the living flame

So, What now?
Where go I?
When you think it's all said and
done

Venom of a life insane
Bites into your fragile vein

Internalize and decimate
Patronize and complicate

So, What now?
Where go I?
When you think it's all said and
done

Bow down
Sell your soul to me
I will set you free
Pacify your demons
Bow down
Surrender unto me
Submit infectiously
Sanctify your demons

Into abyss
You don't exist
Cannot resist
The Judas kiss

Judas lives, recite this vow
I've become your new God now

Followed you from dawn of time
Whispered thoughts into your
mind

Watched your towers hit the
ground
Lured your children never found
Helped your kings abuse their
crown

In the heart of feeble man
Plant the seed of my own plan

The strong and powerful will fall
Find a piece of me in all…
Inside you all

So, Bow down
Sell your soul to me
I will set you free
Pacify your demons
Bow down
Surrender unto me
Submit infectiously
Sanctify your demons

Into abyss
You don't exist
Cannot resist
The Judas kiss

MY APOCALYPSE

Claustrophobic
Crawl out of this skin

Heart explosive
Reach in, pull that pin

Fear thy name, extermination
Desecrate inhale the fire

So we cross that line
Into the grips
Total eclipse
Suffer unto my apocalypse

Deadly vision
Prophecy reveal

Death magnetic
Pulling closer still

Fear thy name, annihilation
Desolate inhale the fire

So we cross that line
Into the grips
Total eclipse
Suffer unto my apocalypse

Crushing metal, ripping skin
Tossing body, mannequin
Spilling blood, bleeding gas

Mangle flesh, snapping spine
Dripping bloody valentine
Shatter face, spitting glass
Split apart
Split apart
Split apart
Spit
Spit it out

What makes me drift a little bit
closer?
Dead man takes the steering
wheel
What makes me know its time
to cross over?
Born to repeat until I feel

See through the skin, bones they
all rattle
Future and past, they disagree
Flesh falls away, bones they all
scatter
I start to see the end in me

Claustrophobic
Climb out of this skin

Heart explosive
Reach in, pull that pin

Violate, annihilate
All wounds unto my eyes

Obliterate, exterminate
As life itself denied

Fear thy name as hell awakens
Destiny inhale the fire

But we've crossed that line
Into the grips
Total eclipse
Suffer unto my apocalypse

Tyrant awaken my apocalypse
Demon awaken my apocalypse
Heaven awaken my apocalypse
Suffer forever my apocalypse

HARDWIRED...
TO SELF-DESTRUCT

HARDWIRED

In the name of desperation
In the name of wretched pain
In the name of all creation gone insane

We're so fucked
Shit out of luck
Hardwired to self-destruct. Go!

On the way to paranoia
On the crooked borderline
On the way to great destroyer, doom design

We're so fucked
Shit out of luck
Hardwired to self-destruct. Oh!

Once upon a planet burning, once upon a flame
Once upon a fear returning, all in vain
Do you feel that hope is fading?
Do you comprehend?
Do you feel it terminating in the end?

We're so fucked
Shit out of luck
Hardwired to self-destruct
Hardwired to self-destruct
Self-destruct
Self-destruct
Self-destruct

ATLAS, RISE!

Bitterness and burden, curses
rest on thee
Solitaire and sorrow, all Eternity
Save the earth and claim
perfection
Deem the mass and blame
rejection
Hold the pose, feign perception
Grudges break your back

All you bear
All you carry
All you bear
Place it right on, right on me

Die as you suffer in vain
Own all the grief and the pain
Die as you hold up the skies
Atlas, Rise!
How does it feel on your own?
Bound by the world all alone
Crushed under heavy skies
Atlas, Rise!

Crucify and witness, circling
the sun
Bastardize and ruin, what have
you become?
Blame the world and blame your
maker
Wish 'em to the undertaker
Crown yourself the other savior
So you carry on

All you bear
All you carry
All you bear
Place it right on, right on me

Die as you suffer in vain
Own all the grief and the pain
Die as you hold up the skies
Atlas, Rise!
How does it feel on your own?
Bound by the world all alone
Crushed under heavy skies
Crushed under heavy skies
Atlas, Rise!

Masquerade as maker, heavy is
the crown
Beaten down and broken, drama
wears you down
Overload, the martyr stumbles
Hit the ground and heaven
crumbles
All alone the fear shall humble
Swallow all your pride

All you bear
All you carry
All you bear
Place it right on, right on me

Die as you suffer in vain
Own all the grief and the pain
Die as you hold up the skies
Atlas, Rise!
How does it feel on your own?
Bound by the world all alone
Crushed under heavy skies
Crushed under heavy skies
Atlas, Rise!

NOW THAT WE'RE DEAD

When the darkness falls, may it be that we should see the light
When reaper calls, may it be that we walk straight and right
When doubt returns, may it be that faith shall permeate our scars
When we're seduced, then may it be that we not deviate our cause

All sinners, a future
All saints, a past
Beginning, the ending
Return to ash

Now that we're dead, my dear, we can be together
Now that we're dead, my dear, we can live forever

When all is pain, may it be it's all we've ever known
When flame consumes, may it be it warms our dying bones
When loss has won, may it be it's you I'm madly fighting for
When Kingdom comes, may it be we walk right through that open door

All sinners, a future
All saints, a past
Beginning, the ending
Return to ash

Now that we're dead, my dear, we can be together
Now that we're dead, my dear, we can live forever

All sinners, a future
All saints, a past
Beginning, the ending
Return to ash

Now that we're dead, my dear, we can be together
Now that we're dead, my dear, we can live, we can live forever

Return to ashes, shed this skin
Beyond the black, we rise again
We shall love forever

MOTH INTO FLAME

Blacked out, pop queen, amphetamine
The screams crashed into silence
Tapped out, doused in the gasoline
The high times going timeless
Decadence, death of the innocence
The pathway starts to spiral
Infamy all for publicity
Destruction going viral

Light it up, ah, light it up
Another hit erases all the pain
Bulletproof, ah, kill the truth
You're falling, but you think you're flying high
High again

Sold your soul, built a higher wall
Yesterday, now you're thrown away
Same rise and fall
Who cares at all?
Seduced by fame, a moth into the flame

Twisted, backstabbing, wicked, the delusion absolution
Perjurer, fame is the murderer, seduce you into ruin

Light it up, ah, light it up
Another hit erases all the pain
Bulletproof, ah, tell the truth
You're falling, but you think you're flying high
High again

Sold your soul, built a higher wall
Yesterday, now you're thrown away
Same rise and fall
Who cares at all?
Seduced by fame, a moth into the flame
Burn!

Guarantee your name, you go and kill yourself
The vultures feast around you still
Overdose on shame and insecurity
If one won't do, that fistful will

Death scene, black hearse, the limousine, a grave filled with seduction
Vaccine, fame does the murdering. She builds up for destruction

So we light it up, ah, light it up
Another hit erases all the pain
Bulletproof, ah, no excuse
You're falling, but you think you're flying high
High again

Sold your soul, built a higher wall
Yesterday, now you're thrown away
Same rise and fall
Who cares at all?
Seduced by fame, a moth into the flame
Addicted to the fame

DREAM NO MORE

He sleeps under black seas waiting, lies dreaming in death
He sleeps under cosmos shaking, stars granting his breath
He wakes as the world dies screaming, all horrors arrive
He wakes giving Earth its bleeding, pure madness alive

And He haunts you
And He binds your soul
And He loathes you
And reclaims it all

You turn to stone, can't look away
You turn to stone, madness they say
Cthulu awaken

He sways in abyss returning, inhaling black skies
He shakes with a torture burning, all lost in His eyes

And He haunts you
And He binds your soul
And He loathes you
And reclaims it all

You turn to stone, can't look away
You turn to stone, madness they say
Cthulu awaken

You turn to stone, can't look away
You turn to stone, madness they say
Sanity taken, seething damnation
Cthulu awaken
Winged salvation, death by creation
Cthulu awaken (Wake!)
Dreaming no more
Cthulu awaken (Wake!)
Dreaming no more

HALO ON FIRE

Obey, obey. Come, won't you stay?
Sincere, sincere. All ends in tears
Endure, endure. Thoughts most impure
Concede, concede. But both shall we bleed?

Oh! Halo on fire, the midnight knows it well
Fast is desire, creates another hell
I fear to turn on the light, for the darkness won't go away
Fast is desire
Turn out the light
Halo on fire

Allure, allure. Sweetness obscure
Abide, abide. Secrets inside
Deprive, deprive to feel more alive
Obey, obey. Just don't turn away

Oh! Halo on fire, the midnight knows it well
Fast is desire, creates another hell
I fear to turn on the light, for the darkness won't go away
Fast is desire
Turn out the light
Halo on fire

Prayers cannot get through, return to sender
Unto which of you shall I surrender?
Twisting in disguise, dark resurrection
Lighting up the skies, wicked perfection
Too dark to sleep, can't slip away
Open or close, my eyes betray
Beyond the black
Come, won't you stay?

Hello darkness, say goodbye
Hello darkness, say goodbye

CONFUSION

Wake to face the day, grab this life and walk away
War is never done, rub the patch and battle on
Make it go away
Please make it go away

Confusion, all sanity is now beyond me
Delusion, all sanity is but a mem'ry
My life…the war that never ends

Leave the battlefield, yet its horrors never heal
Coming home from war, pieces don't fit anymore
Make it go away, please make it go away

Confusion, all sanity is now beyond me
Delusion, all sanity is but a mem'ry
My life…the war that never ends

Father, please come home
Shell-shocked, all I've known
Father, please come home

Label him a deadwood soldier now, cast away and left to roam
Rapid is the road to sacrifice, just takes longer to come home
Come home

Confusion, all sanity is now beyond me
Delusion, crossfire ricochets inside me
Trapped in a memory forever
My life…the war that never ends

MANUNKIND

Chaos, awaiting for Adam's return
Madness, smiling as we watch it burn

I've become hostage to my mind
Left myself behind
Blind lead blind, quest to find
Faith in man(un)kind

Garden of Eden, so simple and pure
Greedy, needy, must we have more?

I've become hostage to my mind
Left myself behind
Blind lead blind, quest to find
Faith in man(un)kind

Fascinate, part of insanity
Decimate, lessons we never learn
Dominate, killing of the innocence
Deviate, and to dust you return
Yeah

Seized by the day, frozen captive by the night
Seized by the day, all the dark days of your life

Seized by the day, frozen captive by the night
Led so astray, all the dark days of your life

Zero, reset, creation of man
Foolish, ready to witness again?
I've become hostage to my mind
Left myself behind
Blind lead blind, quest to find
Faith in man(un)kind
Faith in man(un)kind
Faith in man(un)kind
Faith in man(un)kind
Oh, faith in man(un)kind

HERE COMES REVENGE

Little grave I'm grieving, I will
mend you
Sweet revenge I'm dreaming
I will end you
I've been here since dawn of
time
Countless hatreds built my shrine
I was born in anger's flame
He was Abel, I was Cain
I am here, I'm hell unbound
Burn your kingdom to the
ground, to the ground

Here comes revenge, just for you
Revenge, you can't undo
Revenge, is killing me
Revenge, set me free
Eye for an eye, tooth for a tooth
A life for a life, it's my burden
of proof
Revenge, just for you
Revenge
You ask forgiveness, I give you
sweet revenge

I return this nightmare, I will find
you
Sleepless, cloaked in despair, I'm
behind you
Man has made me, oh, so strong
Blurring lines of right and wrong
Far too late for frail amends
Now it's come to sweet revenge
Desp'rate hands that lose control
Have no mercy on your soul, on
your soul

Here comes revenge, just
for you
Revenge, you can't undo
Revenge, is killing me
Revenge, just set me free
Eye for an eye, tooth for a tooth
A life for a life, it's my burden
of proof
Revenge, just for you
Revenge
You ask forgiveness, I give you
sweet revenge

Here comes revenge, just
for you
Revenge, you can't undo
Revenge, is killing me
Revenge, set me free
Eye for an eye, tooth for a tooth
A life for a life, it's my burden
of proof
Revenge, just for you
Revenge
You ask forgiveness, I give you
sweet revenge
Sweet revenge

AM I SAVAGE?

Ooh, run away, the past will
bite again
Ooh, no matter where you dwell
You, here again, a captive of
the howl
You, welcome back to hell

Faithful as the full moon is rising
Beauty and the Beast are colliding
Sharpened edge touch liquid
flame
Deepened seed soaks anger's
reign
Arching back shape-shift
derange
Father, how I watched you
change

Am I savage?
Scratching at the door
Am I savage?
I don't recognize you anymore

Ooh, tooth is fang, twisting
under skin
Ooh, foul tongue, black breath
Change, snap inside, the Beast
about complete
Change, soon infects the rest

Faithful as the full moon is rising
Beauty and the Beast are
colliding
Sharpened edge touch liquid
flame
Deepened seed soaks anger's
reign
Arching back shape-shift
derange
Father, how I watched you
change

Am I savage?
Howling at the door
Am I savage?
I don't recognize you anymore
Anymore

Ooh, inheritance, the past has
bit again
Ooh, the next heir or anarchy
Feel stretching skin, so far
beyond belief
I feel the ever-changing you
in me

Am I savage?
Scratching at the door
Am I savage?
Howling evermore
Am I savage?
I don't recognize me anymore
Anymore
Anymore. Ha, ha, ha
Am I savage?

MURDER ONE

One crown shines on through the sound
One crown, born to lose
One man does not give a damn
One man, no excuse
Aces wild, aces high
All the aces, aces 'til you die

White lines fading, the iron horse rolls on and on and on

Hear your thunder, still feeding back
Still hear your thunder
The man in black, born to lose, living to win

One fist hammers through the mist
One fist, steady on
One heart, die hard from the start
One heart beats its song
Murder all, murder one
Gimme murder, second class to none

Headlights fading, the iron horse rolls on and on and on

Hear your thunder, still feeding back
Still hear your thunder
The man in black, born to lose, living to win

Hear your thunder, still feeding back
I still hear your thunder
The man in black, born to lose, no excuse
Til the end, been living to win
Been living to win

SPIT OUT THE BONE

Come unto me and you will feel perfection
Come unto me and dedicate
Come unto me, you'll never feel rejection
Come unto me and terminate
Remove your heart, it's only good for bleeding
Bleeding through your fragile skin

Disappear, like a man was never here

Long live machine, the future supreme
Man overthrown, spit out the bone

Plug into me, I guarantee devotion
Plug into me and dedicate
Plug into me, I'll save you from emotion
Plug into me and terminate
Accelerate, utopian solution
Fin'lly cure the earth of man
Exterminate, speeding up the evolution
Set on a course, a master plan

Reinvent the earth inhabitant

Long live machine, the future supreme
Man overthrown, spit out the bone

The flesh betrays the flesh
Your man has had his time
We lay him down to rest
Machine, the new divine

Stop breathing and dedicate to me (Dedicate to me)
Stop dreaming and terminate for me (Terminate for me)
All meaning you dedicate to me (Dedicate to me)
All feelings you terminate for me

Disappear, like a man was never here

Long live machine, our future supreme
Your man overthrown, spit out the bone
Yeah

PERMISSIONS

Notice of songwriters is given, followed by song title and year of copyright.

Words and Music by James Hetfield: "Motorbreath" (1983).

Words and Music by James Hetfield and Lars Ulrich: "Ain't My Bitch" (1996); "Am I Savage?" (2016); "Atlas, Rise!" (2016); "Attitude" (1997); "Battery" (1986); "Better Than You" (1997); "Confusion" (2016); "Cure" (1996); "Devil's Dance" (1997); "Don't Tread on Me" (1991); "Dream No More" (2016); "The God That Failed" (1991); "Halo on Fire" (2016); "Hardwired" (2016); "Harvester of Sorrow" (1988); "Here Comes Revenge" (2016); "Hit the Lights" (1983); "Holier Than Thou" (1991); "I Disappear" (2000); "Leper Messiah" (1986); "Low Man's Lyric" (1997); "Mama Said" (1996); "The Memory Remains" (1997); "- Human" (1999); "Moth into Flame" (2016); "Murder One" (2016); "No Leaf Clover" (1999); "No Remorse" (1983); "Nothing Else Matters" (1991); "Now That We're Dead" (2016); "One" (1988); "The Outlaw Torn" (1996); "Poor Twisted Me" (1996); "Prince Charming" (1997); "Ronnie" (1996); "Sad but True" (1991); "Seek & Destroy" (1983); "The Shortest Straw" (1988); "Spit Out the Bone" (2016); "The Struggle Within" (1991); "Until It Sleeps" (1996); "Wherever I May Roam" (1991); "Whiplash" (1983).

Words and Music by James Hetfield, Lars Ulrich and Cliff Burton: "Fight Fire with Fire" (1984); "For Whom the Bell Tolls" (1984); "To Live Is to Die" (1988).

Words and Music by James Hetfield, Lars Ulrich, Cliff Burton and Kirk Hammett: "Creeping Death" (1984); "Fade to Black" (1984).

Words and Music by James Hetfield, Lars Ulrich, Cliff Burton and Dave Mustaine: "Ride the Lightning" (1984).

Words and Music by James Hetfield, Lars Ulrich and Kirk Hammett: "...And Justice for All" (1988); "Bad Seed" (1997); "Bleeding Me" (1996); "Carpe Diem Baby" (1997); "Disposable Heroes" (1986); "Dyers Eve" (1988); "Enter Sandman" (1991); "Escape" (1984); "Eye of the Beholder" (1988); "Fixxxer" (1997); "The Frayed Ends of Sanity" (1988); "Fuel" (1997); "Hero of the Day" (1996); "The House Jack Built" (1996); "King Nothing" (1996); "Of Wolf and Man" (1991); "Slither" (1997); "The Thing That Should Not Be" (1986); "The Thorn Within" (1996); "Through the Never" (1991); "Trapped Under Ice" (1984); "2 x 4" (1996); "The Unforgiven" (1991); "The Unforgiven II" (1997); "Wasting My Hate" (1996); "Welcome Home (Sanitarium)" (1986).

Words and Music by James Hetfield, Lars Ulrich, Kirk Hammett and Cliff Burton: "Damage, Inc." (1986); "Master of Puppets" (1986).

Words and Music by James Hetfield, Lars Ulrich and Jason Newsted: "Blackened" (1988); "My Friend of Misery" (1991); "Where the Wild Things Are" (1997).

Words and Music by James Hetfield, Lars Ulrich and Dave Mustaine: "The Four Horsemen" (1983); "Jump in the Fire" (1983); "Metal Militia" (1983); "Phantom Lord" (1983).

Music by Metallica, Lyrics by James Hetfield: "All Nightmare Long" (2008); "Broken, Beat & Scarred" (2008); "Cyanide" (2008); "The Day That Never Comes" (2008); "The End of the Line" (2008); "The Judas Kiss" (2008); "My Apocalypse" (2008); "That Was Just Your Life" (2008); "The Unforgiven III" (2008).

Words and Music by James Hetfield, Lars Ulrich, Kirk Hammett and Bob Rock, Copyright © 2003 Creeping Death Music (GMR), EMI Blackwood (Canada) Music Ltd. and Mahina Hoku Publishing. All Rights for EMI Blackwood (Canada) Music Ltd. and Mahina Hoku Publishing Administered by Sony/ATV Music Publishing LLC, 424 Church Street, Suite 1200, Nashville, TN 37219. International Copyright Secured. All Rights Reserved. "All Within My Hands"; "Dirty Window"; "Frantic"; "Invisible Kid"; "My World"; "Purify"; "St. Anger"; "Shoot Me Again"; "Some Kind of Monster"; "Sweet Amber"; "The Unnamed Feeling".

Words and Music by James Hetfield, Lars Ulrich and Robert Trujillo: "ManUNkind" (2016).

INDEX